PRISONERS OF HOPE

Prisoners of Hope

Sundry Sunday Essays

Steven J. Keillor

REGENT COLLEGE PUBLISHING
Vancouver, British Columbia

Published 2007 by Regent College Publishing
5800 University Boulevard, Vancouver, BC V6T 2E4 Canada
Web: www.regentpublishing.com
E-mail: info@regentpublishing.com

Unless otherwise noted, Scripture quotations are from Today's
New International Version of the Bible, copyright © 2001,
2005 by the International Bible Society. Used by permission of
Zondervan Publishers.

"Jeg fandt en ven" and "Har du intet rum for Jesus?" are taken
from *Salmer og Sange* (København, 1933).

Regent College Publishing is an imprint of the Regent
Bookstore <www.regentbookstore.com>. Views expressed in
works published by Regent College Publishing are those of the
author and do not necessarily represent the official position of
Regent College <www.regent-college.edu>.

Library and Archives Canada Cataloguing in Publication

Keillor, Steven J. (Steven James)
Prisoners of hope : sundry sunday essays / Steven J. Keillor.

Includes bibliographical references.

ISBN-10: 1-57383-070-4
ISBN-13: 978-1-57383-070-6

1. Christianity and culture. 2. Jesus Christ—Meditations.
I. Title.

BR115.C8K42 2007   261   C2007-901409-7

CONTENTS

1

CROSSING BOUNDARIES

This collection of essays and poems represents an attempt to cross some boundaries, so perhaps I should explain the attempt at the outset lest the reader think I am simply being aggressive, angry, or insensitive. Here, an historian and layman essays to write about religious subjects and a Minnesotan is so bold as to criticize Scandinavia, and then compounds the problem by criticizing his own country. I do so because boundaries need to be crossed.

Ours is increasingly a post-Christian society—even where the formalities of church attendance are observed—which confines Christian beliefs to a private world of values, in Lesslie Newbigin's words, while it conducts public debate on its own terms. This confinement Christians can never accept. American public debate is not so enlightened that it has no need for Christian values, nor is Christianity such a shy, private affair that it has nothing to say out in public

I have several personal excuses as well for crossing boundaries. I was raised in the Plymouth Brethren, who recognized no distinction between clergy and laity. At least in their minds, I, as a born-again Christian, am qualified to write about Christ, His Church, and the Gospel. In addition, for most of the past thirteen years I have lived near the small town of Askov, Minnesota; rural people often do not accept urban specialization. Here you can be a fireman, a banker, and a city councilman all at once. Here an historian can write poetry, preach, teach from the Bible, and write travel stories, too.

Also, I have crossed some spiritual boundaries during my life: child of devout parents, serious Bible-reading teen, rebellious college student, InterVarsity member, young man in the Assembly fellowship, near-apostate youth, serious self-doubter, and, now, firm believer in Jesus Christ. If I stress the opposition between the world and the Father, it is because I too have been seduced by the world. If I mention Christ too often, it is because it has taken me so long to really find this Friend. If I criticize the rural American dream, it is because I have so strongly strived to achieve it.

Autobiography proves nothing. So I have tried not to argue on the basis of my own experiences in these essays. To do so would be to confine myself to the private world of values. That I cannot do and still remain faithful to my Lord, Who clearly claims Lordship over the public world as well.

These ideas are completely my own responsibility. Yet I want to gratefully acknowledge my debts to others: to many Christian friends in the Askov-Sandstone-Hinckley area, to Lanny and Kathy Lundquist for the use of their computer, to Dean Carroll for printing this book, to Bob Clark and the InterVarsity graduate students for their ideas and fellowship, to David Heiller for permission to use articles and poems which originally appeared in the *Askov American*, to my wife Margaret and my children— Jeremy, William, and Amanda—who have endured my absence on Sunday afternoons and most of all, to my parents, to whom this book is dedicated and who have suffered the most from my spiritual wrong turns in the past.

2

THE END

The ice floe shipping season
On Rainy River nearly over,
Grinding against advancing shore ice,
Late-starting floes struggle downstream
As the channel closes.

Frigid air encounters open water.
White mists—ethereal as the day-moon
Over Ontario—rise from the river,
And the north wind blows them
Toward the Minnesota bank.

Along the backwaters of the Big Fork,
Wind-blown, in the sub-zero cold,
Dead elms crackle like old men's ankles.
My skis creak like rocking chairs
Rhythmically hitting hardwood.

Dormant hardwoods climb the Grand Mound
Where a thousand Old Years lie buried
Under signs citing a state statute

Against digging them—or the Woodland culture
That flourished here—up again.

December 31st, the site closes for the year.
Heeding the caretaker's note on my windshield,
I close and lock the heavy wooden gate
On the Old Year behind—
The last one out.

3

SERIOUS MISCALCULATIONS

For a people who pride ourselves on our practicality—our constant attention to the "bottom line," we have an amazing way of hiding practical truths from our own eyes. Just as we might turn our heads as we pass by the scene of a serious automobile accident—so we think that we can turn our minds away from our own condition. We persistently refuse to admit to ourselves all of the consequences of our own mortality.

The problem goes beyond an unwillingness to think about death. "Death education" courses can cause people to confront their mortality by encouraging them to talk about it or by having them visit a mortuary. But what is accepted is only the consequences that can be anticipated beforehand: the physical consequences for the body, the separation from all that we have known, the grieving relatives and friends left behind. What is not discussed is what happens to *us* after death.

That is only natural, for we act as if we are children who have stumbled quite by accident onto an amazing world of light and shadows, colors, sounds, things to feel and things to taste—all assembled here quite by accident and left for us to do with as we please without any accountability on our part. Naturally, then, to depart this pleasant scene only means that the story is over—and the colors and sounds are no longer ours to enjoy, that's all.

We seriously miscalculate. We fancy that the living is like singing in the shower—that there is no audience (certainly not a critical audience), no standards of performance, no wrong notes and no singing out of tune. It's all for fun. We do not realize Whose stage it is that we are standing on. We do not realize just what Audience it is that we are speaking our lines to and performing our deeds in front of.

In our ignorance, we are like the Joneses down the block who—totally ignorant of classical music, its history, or the places where it is performed—and thinking they are to give a skit in front of a few friends, suddenly walk out onto the Carnegie Hall stage without any preparation, with Mr. Jones wearing Bermuda shorts and sporting a two-day growth of beard, the whole family whistling "Me and My Shadow" to a shocked sell-out crowd dressed in tuxedos and evening dresses and obviously expecting something quite different, and then closing their performance by waving one finger ("We're Number One!") in the air and saluting the world-famous conductor as "Bud."

Like them, we expect polite approval from a neighborly audience with low expectations, and we will be stunned by the response. We will discover that we have seriously miscalculated.

We have many ways of deceiving ourselves about Who our audience is, what the standards of performance are, and how we can or cannot meet those standards.

In recent years, we Americans have been quite innovative in developing certain symbolic virtues in order to conceal or compensate for our faults. There are numerous charitable causes: we can donate money, or participate in a walkathon and obtain pledges, or donate an hour of our time once a week. We can purchase a pull-tab or a raffle ticket, and thus help a charity while giving ourselves a chance at a sizeable jackpot.

The environmental movement has generated numerous expressions of symbolic virtue: recycling, buying from a company which will donate part of its profits to the environment, refusing to buy polluters' products, and participating in boycotts and marches. It tries to turn our natural appreciation for animals into a symbolic virtue. Created with a capacity and a responsibility to know God Himself, we satisfy ourselves with spending our whole lives getting to know wolves or sled dogs or chimpanzees—His creatures. We make that a symbolic virtue. Yet wouldn't we rather get to know our human father than to spend a lifetime admiring the house he built, even if it had ornate railings and hand-carved nooks and crannies?

How do we create symbolic virtue? We take the standards of morality that we have inherited from past generations. Then we "drain" away the idea of a just and holy God that was associated with that morality. We siphon off any notion of punishment for falling short of the standard. Then we redefine obligations to God to mean mutual obligations to each other as human beings. We focus on the positive, on a few actions that people can do, rather on the many possible violations of the standard or on the common ways that we all fall short of the standard. Then we change the name from morality to ethics, to stress the break with the past.

Though there is much that is good about the symbolic actions themselves, the main purpose of this system of ethics is to make us feel good about ourselves and to help us to avoid examining our lives. Most importantly, the initial act of eliminating our Creator God from our thinking is so immoral and unethical in itself as to render the following concern with ethical fine points quite absurd. It's as if students were to murder the teacher and then sit down to have serious discussions about proper manners in the classroom and how many fingers to hold up when wishing to go to the bathroom. Because this ethics begins with the removal of God and with a too-optimistic appraisal of ourselves, it fails utterly to solve social problems. It doesn't even make the individual virtuous: "All our righteous acts are like filthy rags" (Isaiah 64:6b).

Often, the local "happy talk" TV news shows that come on at 6 PM or 10 PM throw together one story of symbolic virtue after another (symbolic virtue is often telegenic). Firemen rescue kittens from a burning apartment; shoppers buy at the store that donates $1 per purchase to charity; recycled paper is now being used by the local newspaper; donations from around the country have paid for surgery on a local boy's dog. Meanwhile, the city is wracked by crime, drug abuse, homelessness, divorce, broken homes, child abuse and failing schools. But these stories are only covered if there is some positive "angle"—usually a largely symbolic, totally inadequate (but telegenic) attempt to address the city's real problems. We want to feel good about ourselves, so we focus on the positive. We forget that just as physical pain warns us to take remedial action (take our hand off the hot stove), so social problems or individual faults can force us to examine our lives—instead of hiding the symptoms with happy talk and missing the cure.

Both the strength and weakness of symbolic virtue comes from the fact that it is intended to impress other people. It has a strong hold on us because we want to impress others. Especially when we arrive in our mid-thirties, we feel that we have life all figured out—parenting, marriage, work, recreation. To confirm this we seek the friendship of others who also have it all figured out, and we measure ourselves against them rather than against God's standards. The weakness is that those symbolic, human standards will not be the ones we will finally be judged by.

Males measure themselves against other males and conclude that many forms of traditional virtue were simply never meant for males. They develop the "short list" of rules for males. Women measure themselves against the males at the office, and find themselves virtuous by comparison. That conviction is strengthened as they develop close friendships with other females, stress the importance of relationships, and feel virtuous for working on relationships without realizing that they have no relationship at all with the most important Person, their Creator God. Relationships become symbolic virtues.

We act like clever defense attorneys in our use of these symbolic virtues. As we daily stand trial before the jury of our peers with their scrutinizing opinions of us, we realize that they are sentimental, easily distracted, with limited ability (or interest) to understand us, and with limited recall of past events—so we stress some sentimental, symbolic virtues in our closing argument and hope that they will remember these and forget our faults. We hope they will focus on one characteristic—marital faithfulness, control of temper, kindness to strangers—and will forget alcoholism, greed, and cheating on taxes. We forget that our real Audience has unlimited knowledge of us, an unlimited attention span, total recall, and intense interest in every detail of our lives.

When we do admit that God is our Audience and our Judge, we often pride ourselves on the fact that we have a baptismal or confirmation certificate or a certificate of church membership that we can show Him to obtain a favorable verdict. Here we seriously miscalculate. If my wife asked me if I loved her, would

I take the marriage certificate out of the desk drawer as proof positive that I loved her, was faithful to her, and had succeeded with her in building a successful marriage and loving family? Would I show her photographs or a videotape of the marriage ceremony as proof of a loving relationship? Of course not. Yet, we somehow think that the all-knowing God is fooled by long-ago ceremonies, formal rituals, and yellowing documents into thinking that we love Him, serve Him, and obey Him. What might possibly fool a spouse will never fool a God who knows our thoughts and our hearts.

We have even miscalculated our holidays. When we can escape the shopping rush and get ourselves into a reflective, supposedly religious mood, we celebrate Christmas as a happy, family time when we can rejoice in the birth of the little Infant and exchange gifts. The Birth of the Christ Child is seen as only Good News. Of course, it is good news, but, as in the "good news-bad news" jokes, it has its "bad news" side too.

When you are swimming at the public beach and the lifeguard suddenly strips off his shirt and speeds down the ladder from his lifeguard's tower and races across the beach into the water and swims frantically towards you, this is no doubt an inspiring sight and a reassuring indication that someone is interested in your welfare, but it is also Bad News—you are drowning! It is strong proof of that.

When you are sitting around the Christmas tree reading from Luke or Matthew about the shepherds in the fields and the baby in the manger—when you see, as it were, the Son of God stripping away His divine splendor and speeding down from heaven to be born of a virgin and racing to the Cross out of love for you—no doubt this is inspiring and reassuring, but it is also Bad News—you are in danger of going to hell.

We badly miscalculate when we take only the warm, cozy feelings of these two holidays, and ignore the warning that is wrapped up in them. We somehow interpret the Christmas and Easter stories as merely symbolic gestures on God's part—as if He couldn't think of any better way to express His love except by submitting to a birth in a manger and to a death on a crude Roman cross—as if these actions were a sort of parable or story showing us His love, but not necessary actions to save us from eternal punishment—as if His birth and death related only to His love and not also to our danger.

But if these were meant as symbolic gestures, they failed completely. Herod failed to catch the symbolism in Jesus' birth, took literally the news that the King of the Jews (thus, a rival) had been born, and "gave orders to kill all the boys in Bethlehem who were two years old and under" (Matthew 2:16b). To make a merely symbolic gesture which resulted in the death of innocent children seems like a tragic mistake on God's part.

Similarly, the Pharisees took literally Jesus' statement that "'I and the Father are one,'" and they "picked up stones to stone him, "because, they told Him, "'you, a mere man, claim to be God'" (John 10:30, 31b, 33b). The idea of God becoming a man was completely foreign to their religious thinking; the claim of a mere man to be God was blasphemy to them. If the act of God becoming a man was intended as a symbolic gesture demonstrating divine love, then it was an impossible gesture to them, a symbol that made no sense. To non-Jews also, the idea of God becoming a man, then dying a criminal's death on a cross, and rising from the dead was preposterous. After the Apostle Paul told this story, the Roman governor Porcius Festus shouted, "You're out of your mind, Paul! Your great learning is driving you insane" (Acts 26:24b).

Surely, if God only intended to communicate His love in symbolic terms, then this symbol was the wrong one to use, for people did not understand it and thought it foolish. It would have made more sense to those living in the first-century if He had decided to show His love in ways they could understand— for instance, by allowing labor-saving machines, cars and air-conditioning to be invented two millennia early. Or, He could have just sent a little more rain in the growing season and a little less at harvest.

No, our Creator's love to us—in our role as ordinary John and Jane Doe with a family to feed and lives to lead—is constantly expressed in the sunshine and the rain, in growing plants, beautiful sunsets, and rich harvests. That's taken care of, and Christmas and Easter are unnecessary as expressions of that Creator's love. The manger and the cross were needed as expressions of His love towards us as: John & Jan Doe, Sinners, Wanted for Adultery, Lying and Theft.

They are not merely symbolic gestures, but desperately needed acts to save us from the extreme danger we face. Our Audience of One knew we could never come up to His standards and so He provided a stand-in who could.

We have an Audience of One—the Ancient of Days. The prophet Isaiah saw Him "seated on a throne, high and exalted. The train of His robe filled the temple" and the voices of His attendants shook the temple. Isaiah cried, "Woe is me! I am ruined! For I am a man of unclean lips, and I live among a people of unclean lips, and my eyes have seen the King, the Lord Almighty" (Isaiah 6:1b, 4–5).

> Daniel also saw Him in a vision:
> . . . and the Ancient of Days took His seat.
> His clothing was white as snow; the hair of His head was white like wool.
> His throne was flaming with fire, and its wheels were all ablaze.

A river of fire was flowing, coming out from before Him.
Thousands upon thousands attended Him; ten thousand times
ten thousand stood before Him.
The court was seated, and the books were opened.
(Daniel 7:9b–10)

An absolutely perfect, holy God who can not bear to look upon evil is on His throne.

Here is where we come sauntering in, as it were, waving and saying "Hi, God!" only to find that we have seriously miscalculated our situation. There we stand with silly clichés on our lips:

I've lived a long life and I'm ready to go;
You can only go around once—I've had my chance;
Nobody's perfect and I'm better than most;
I've been true to myself and that's what counts

—only to find thick books being opened and unbelievably detailed accounts of our actions, thoughts and words being read out loud for all to hear, and the Most High giving His most solemn attention to the reading—as if preparing to deliver a solemn sentence of judgment after the long account is read. It's Carnegie Hall and we've come in our shorts.

And with what is doing, the darkness of the night, the solemnity
of the place, and of the occasion, and conscious guilt, all conspire
to make terror thrill through every power of the soul, and rouse
it to awful attention.

God has provided a way for us to be delivered from the solemn sentence of judgment:

But God demonstrates His own love for us in this: While we
were still sinners, Christ died for us. Since we have now been
justified by His blood, how much more shall we be saved from
God's wrath through Him! (Romans 5:8–9)

I saw a notice posted on a college teacher's file cabinet—one of these humorous notices photocopied and passed around at the office. It read,

> This Life is a Test and Only a Test.
> If This was Your Real Life
> You Would Have Been Given Better Instructions.

This *is* your real life, and you *have* been given good instructions in the Scriptures, the Word of God. These instructions have not been given *in case of emergency.* Your life *is* an Emergency, a real Emergency. Turn to the instructions.

In the sixteenth chapter of Acts, the jailer at Philippi was faced with an emergency—the prison doors were opened and he was sure to be executed if any prisoners escaped. He prepared to commit suicide to forestall his execution. Then he discovered that the prisoners, Paul and Silas, were still there, so the emergency should have been over. Yet the jailer must have seen the deeper emergency that was his life itself, for he "fell trembling before Paul and Silas" and "asked, 'Sirs, what must I do to be saved?'" Paul and Silas answered, "'Believe in the Lord Jesus, and you will be saved.'" The jailer did believe and both emergencies were ended, for he "brought them into his house and set a meal before them; he was filled with joy because he had come to believe in God—he and his whole family" (Acts 16:26–34).

See your life as an Emergency. The above-quoted passage about "the darkness of the night" and "the solemnity of the place, and of the occasion" does not describe God's judgment but rather the famous Cane Ridge revival of August 1801. Alarmed at their emergency, many roused their soul "to awful attention" and then experience "raptures of joy" when they experience deliverance. "Always, or almost always," the awful attention led to "unparalleled joy and happiness."[1]

Don't sit down for another holiday meal of pretended carefree joy while this underlying emergency still confronts you. Don't satisfy your conscience with symbolic virtues. Don't imagine that the opinions that count are those of your fallible, forgetful, often foolish co-workers and peers. Deal with the real emergency in your life—the fact that your "performance" in life cannot satisfy your Audience of One.

It was this emergency that brought the Christ Child to the manger and to the cross. Only His life and death satisfied your Righteous Judge, and through faith you must accept Him as your substitute if you are to escape God's judgment.

4

OUR FAMOUS BROTHER

(December 25, 1988)

I just have a few words to say
On this, my Brother's birthday.
I will be brief and soon sit down again.
Let the celebration continue then.

Someone I have Hero-worshipped for years
I can't quite see as a baby, cooing or in tears,
But as a Hero, using just the right touch of irony
(Like Gary) to show people they had misspoken badly;
Or, leading the way to His execution site
While His brothers hung back from fright;
Or, after He rose again, by the sea shore
Cooking breakfast for His brothers,
Like Phil in the Boundary Waters.
(Was He always up first in the morning?)

We needed more than a baby, a hero or a king.
We had squandered our inheritance on squalid things.
If there had been more left we would have sold that too.

Only a close relative, by law, could buy us back
And He became our nearest relative to do just that.

This talk doesn't deal with babies, but then
It isn't only babies that are born.
And, I'm not sure the Father is as involved when
We're babies (most fathers aren't) as when
The children or adults can talk and understand.
Then He tells them of His plan,
Asks if they will take their Brother's hand,
And be born into the Father's family.
These birthdays—more than His own—
Their famous Brother loves to see:
"Here am I, and the children God has given Me."

5

THAT SCARECROW WORD,
FUNDAMENTALISM

The word "fundamentalism" has become the great scarecrow word of modern American society—used by journalists, politicians, and coffee shop commentators to short-circuit thought and frighten people away from considering unpleasant realities or accepting amazing grace. It is a label attached to certain opinions and their spokespersons: WARNING—EXPIRATION DATE July 1925—DO NOT CONSUME. With this label, the individual does not have to "taste and see" in order to know the contents. The label discourages tasting and seeing.

Our culture derives this scarecrow word primarily from the portrayal of 1920s fundamentalism in American history textbooks and popular journalism. The standard account culminates in the supposed defeat of fundamentalism at the Scopes trial in Dayton, Tennessee, in July 1925. With this caricature engraved on our national consciousness, we have proceeded to project it on to other phenomena—for example, Muslim groups who also preach abstention from alcohol and avoidance of sexual promiscuity.

We must first ask the question whether the term "fundamentalist" remains at all useful. When we stretch the word to cover both Bible Belt Christians in Tennessee and Muslim "fundamentalists" in the holy city of Qom, Iran, perhaps we have stretched it beyond the breaking point. If there is anyone whom William Jennings Bryan did not resemble during the Scopes Trial, it was the Ayatollah Khomeini. If we use the word "fundamentalist" to mean anyone who takes their particular creed literally, we are placing together quite different creeds. Surely, the content of the creed matters as much as the distinction between taking the creed literally and interpreting it figuratively.

When we use the word to describe positions taken in current political debates, things become more confusing. As several prominent religious leaders associated themselves with the Republican party during the Reagan-Bush era, we commonly used the word "fundamentalist" to describe the right wing of the Republican party. Yet aid to the contras bore no logical relationship to the content of Christian fundamentalism, and many Christian fundamentalists have always opposed participation in partisan politics.

Whether it's a misleading synonym for "literalist," a scarecrow word, or a shorthand expression for a right-wing fanatic, the term "fundamentalist" badly needs to be more carefully understood.

The movement called fundamentalism began in the early 20th century with a defense of certain "Fundamentals" of the Christian faith: the authenticity of the Bible as the Word of God, the literal truth of Jesus' claim to be the Son of God, the necessity of faith in His sacrificial death for human salvation, and so forth. Several scholars defended these doctrines in a series of pamphlets collectively called *The Fundamentals: A Testimony to the Truth* (1910–1915).[1]

Note that these Fundamentals deal with the claims of Jesus Christ—either claims about His Person or claims He made about the Scriptures. What is ironic (and tragic) is that when we discuss "fundamentalism" today, we discuss everything except the Fundamentals, everything except Jesus Christ. We judge the movement to defend the basics on every other basis except those basics it was meant to defend.

Partly, that is the fault of those fundamentalists who were captured by their own culture and who mistakenly defended certain 19th-century, small-town American values such as white racial supremacy, capitalistic individualism, and abstinence from tobacco or liquor—in addition to defending the Fundamentals. By their statements, they created the impression among some that the Christian faith began in Alabama. Actually, it began in a very cosmopolitan Roman Empire, and flourished in the cosmopolitan cities (Corinth, Philippi, Ephesus, Colosse) in that Empire—not in small backwaters of rural ignorance and prejudice. Today, the revivals in Africa and South Korea are ample evidence that Christianity is well able to win converts across cultural and racial barriers.

Some secular writers add to the misunderstanding by making "Puritanism" a synonym for fundamentalism, and suggesting that Puritanical "uptight"-ness about personal morality, especially sexual morality, is a peculiarly American obsession. We see Puritan pronouncements—and the graffiti defying them—written on the walls of the cave of our national consciousness, and make the odd assumption that such decrees do not exist in the world outside. Quite the opposite is true. The ancient Hebrews were very fastidious about sexual morality; to be stoned to death was one prescribed penalty for adultery.

Whether to Israelites in exile in Egypt, to first century believers in Corinth, to eighteenth century Moravian pietists, to the first British Methodists, to Danes during the *vækkelser* (awakenings) of the early nineteenth century, or to born-again Baby Boomers in late twentieth century America, God has always revealed Himself as holy and absolutely intolerant towards immorality. That's not fundamentalism, it's the only alternative to paganism. That's not an American "hang-up"—it's found throughout the record of God's dealings with humanity.

Secular journalists, historians and commentators contribute to the misunderstanding of fundamentalism by overemphasing its short-term cultural and political agenda, and overlooking the Fundamentals themselves. They have ignored the reality that the Fundamentals far transcend any one nation, culture or political party. Journalists and historians often trivialize religious matters. They focus on cowboy evangelists or Elmer Gantry, but ignore the serious challenge that the Christian gospel poses to the moral laxity and materialistic idolatry of modern society.

The popular emphasis on the "thou shalt nots" of fundamentalism is a highly revealing indicator of the misplaced priorities of modern secular society. It reveals much about American popular culture and very little about fundamentalism.

The "thou shalt nots" were certainly not the primary emphasis in my own fundamentalist upbringing. I was raised by fundamentalist parents and experienced all the well-known consequences: we could not go to movies; we could not dance; we could not smoke or drink; we could not go to ball games on Sundays; we could not swear or tell dirty jokes; we could not be sexually active before or outside of marriage. These restrictions are well-known components of fundamentalism, as it is caricatured in American popular culture.

That not going to the movies, not attending dances, and not reading the more profane works in the modern literary canon are the most emphasized features of fundamentalism, tells us much about our culture-bound, self-absorbed, narcissistic society. Books, magazine articles, reviews, movies—all bounce off the walls of our culture and rebound within its self-contained boundaries. It is racketball more than it is reality. Books are made into movies and then both are reviewed and the reviews themselves are collected into books and they are reviewed—and then twenty or thirty years later all are recycled as we are hit by a wave of nostalgia for that particular decade—and then the nostalgia itself is analyzed in a punning style in the Sunday newspapers.

To such a society, what is incomprehensible is to ignore all of this cultural output. Not just to have not seen the movie but to not believe in seeing movies—that is surprising and, therefore, newsworthy. Man bites dog. Fundamentalist will not view movies.

What are trite cliches to such a society are the fundamental questions of human existence: where did we come from; why are we here; what is right and wrong behavior; what is the Creator like; what happens to us after we die; how can we escape His punishment for our wrong behavior? What I remember vividly from my own childhood are the profound answers that were given to these questions—answers that reached far back into human history, far forward into the future, far beyond us to every human society across the globe, yet deep within to the individual's inner spirit.

But to a self-absorbed society, the only questions are trivial ones. Who played Wally Cleaver in "Leave It To Beaver?" Who wrote *A Connecticut Yankee in King Arthur's Court*? Who was the Democratic nominee in the 1924 presidential election? Who was Elizabeth Taylor's favorite husband? How does Princess Di raise her children? To such questions, who needs answers? "Has not God made foolish the wisdom of the world?" (I Corinthians 1:20b)

What is essential is the Person of Jesus Christ, and the Fundamentals focus on Him: His incarnation as Son of God and Son of Man, His sacrificial death on the Cross, His resurrection and His Second Coming. These essentials are not newsworthy to secular journalists or to talk show hosts or to coffee-shop conversationalists. The who, what, when, where, and why have already been reported, though the details are fading from our cultural memory. A plausible rebuttal, a swoon-on-the-cross story, an exact date for the Shroud of Turin—these are newsworthy. Surely the Fundamentals are not the real story, not the items to put in the lead paragraph. And yet they are.

Why are these Fundamentals essential, and therefore newsworthy? Because they are the only answer to our tragic human condition, an answer that comes from an external Authority and not an answer that we have dreamed up ourselves. Why was fundamentalism necessary? Because religious liberalism was denying the authoritativeness of the answer and claiming that it was merely a cultural artifact of human design and subject to human amendment.

A scholarly criticism of fundamentalism reveals the necessity for it. In his book titled simply *Fundamentalism* (American edition, 1978), Professor James Barr sarcastically asserts that "the Bible in fundamentalism is comparable to the virgin Mary in Roman Catholicism." It is perfect, it is important to salvation, and it cannot be subjected to critical appraisal but must be simply believed. He draws a contrast between belief in Jesus Christ and belief in the Bible. The following passage from Barr's book is revealing:

Thus, amusingly, fundamentalist faith, though concentrated on
the Bible, would not have been possible during the biblical period
itself. The biblical writers were only persons then. The objective
written and external fixed authority that fundamentalists now
revere did not then exist. A fundamentalist, thrown back into
the time of Isaiah or of St. Paul, would have had to meet them as
persons, "subjectively," without the external objectified scripture
that he now depends on.[2]

Though this is delivered as a brilliant *coup de grace* that
demolishes fundamentalism, it is actually an unintended defense
of fundamentalism.

True, fundamentalism "would not have been possible during
the biblical period itself," but more importantly, *it would not
have been needed.* The most important biblical period is the
three-year ministry of Jesus of Nazareth. With the Word-made-
flesh amongst them, who needed an inerrant account of His
deeds and words? When the Bridegroom is present, who will be
off in another room reading the (literal and inerrant) biography
of Him? When the Bridegoom is gone, then there will be need
of trustworthy biographical accounts.

The disciples' awe, the crowds' amazement, at Jesus' sayings
and doings are ample evidence that they did regard Him, while
present with them, as the "objective . . . and external fixed
authority." The fact that His authority was verbal and not
"written" at this point did not make it any less authoritative.
Concerning His early preaching in the Capernaum synagogue,
Mark wrote, "The people were amazed at his teaching, because
he taught them as one who had authority, not as the teachers
of the law" (Mark 1:22a). Unlike contemporary "teachers of the
law," Jesus of Nazareth evidently did not cautiously buttress
his statements with footnotes refering to previous human
commentators, but simply stated them authoritatively.

"External objectified" authoritativeness is not something imposed after the fact by fundamentalists on the Gospel accounts. It is something present from the beginning in them, and claimed by them. It is something essential to this Christian answer to our flawed human condition, for if we had dreamed up the answer it too would be flawed. Only if the answer comes from an external, objective authority, can it in fact be an answer at all.

The Christian answer, which is really God's answer, is unpopular because it exposes our human flaws and errors and teaches our helplessness to save ourselves. For that reason many hate it. But, in a nominally Christian society, they cannot find it difficult to directly attack the Person of Jesus Christ; therefore, their attack on Christianity is instead directed at a caricatured "literalism" or Puritanism or narrowmindedness. These are easier targets.

What will trip up these critics in the end is not the fundamentalist positions on abortion, sexual morality, or evolution. Even in the United States, fundamentalists do not have the political power to dictate government positions on these issues for very long. They cannot convince sinners to consistently vote against sin. The critics realistically refuse to tremble at fundamentalists' supposed political clout.

Yet God Himself has set up a paradoxical reality that will trip up the critics. "The stone the builders rejected has become the capstone . . . A stone that causes men to stumble and a rock that makes them fall" (1 Peter 2:7b–8a). That fundamental capstone or cornerstone is Christ. It is the Christ affirmed in the Fundamentals Who will cause the critics to fall and stumble. For that reason alone, they had best concentrate on the Fundamentals rather on the fundamentalists.

The paradoxical reality is that the world has rejected Him, but God has highly honored Him. (An accurate and fair-minded fundamentalist would not blame the Jewish people alone for this rejection, for He was executed by Roman authority and Gentiles are equally implicated in His death.) The reality is that He will triumph. The amazing grace comes to all who believe in Him and accept God's view of Him rather than the view held by the world. "Fundamentalism" was a necessary defense of this amazing grace and of this amazing Person, not primarily an attempt to legislate cultural deprivation. Don't allow this scarecrow word to keep you away from Him!

MESSIAH'S COME, JERUSALEM

Bravely up Judean hills,
Leading fearful men
To Jerusalem,
Saying they will crucify Him,
Messiah comes, Jerusalem.

High upon Mount Olivet,
The Man of Sorrows says,
"O Jerusalem,
They'll come and strike your temple then."
Messiah weeps, Jerusalem.

Out beyond King Herod's walls,
Carrying a cross,
To the place of skulls—
"Daughters, do not weep for me"—
Messiah falls, Jerusalem.

Tightly sealed in Joseph's tomb,
Lay Israel's hope,

The Son of Man,
Then he bursts into the upper room,
Messiah lives Jerusalem.

High upon Mount Olivet,
On a Day of days,
He receives our praise,
And Israel's daughters shout, "He's come!"
"Messiah's come!" Jerusalem.

THE FOUR PRINCIPLES OF THE APOCALYPSE

The countdown towards the January 15, 1991 deadline and the war in the Persian Gulf turned many Americans' attention very briefly toward the biblical prophecies of Armageddon. Under a front-page headline "A Prelude to Armageddon?" the *Minnesota Daily* (16 January 1991) quoted from Jesus' Olivet discourse on the last days and interviewed pastors, professors and students about the possibility that the prophecy was about to be fulfilled.

A month later, the *Star Tribune* (13 February 1991, p.23A) ran an op-ed piece ("There's a War in the Mideast but it's not the End of the World") that ridiculed the "apocalyptic nonsense" allegedly peddled by best-selling authors such as Hal Lindsey and John Walvoord. It was nonsense because events had supposedly not worked out the way that Walvoord and Lindsey indicated they would in their books on biblical prophecy and current events.

Applying biblical prophecy to specific events has proven hazardous in the past. Yet skeptics often use their *a priori* assumption that correct prophecy is impossible in order to categorically rule out any application at all. The best-selling authors have often succumbed to the temptation to link specific events to specific biblical prophecies instead of concentrating on underlying principles and basic trends. The skeptics have often gone for the cheap debater's points—those few mistaken details—and have missed the main, underlying points, such as the existence of the nation of Israel.

The very existence of the nation of Israel should give any honest skeptic pause. A people driven from their homeland, scattered among the nations almost 2000 years ago, persecuted, pressured to mix and intermarry with their neighbors—they have retained their language, religion and identity, and now have reclaimed their nationhood.

Believers in biblical prophecy predicted back in the mid-19th century that a nation of Israel would be re-established in the land of Palestine, as part of the events leading up to the Second Coming of Christ. People scoffed at the notion. How could a then-obscure corner of the Turkish empire be of more importance for the world's future than the world's greatest power, Great Britain, or the rapidly growing New World democracy, the United States? Yet it is.

Concentrate on the underlying principles of prophecy.

Basic principle #1: God punctures human pretensions. The Western capitalist world discovers that the true cockpit of history is not Europe or Japan or America—places with important *stock exchanges* at least—but the Middle East and the tiny nation of Israel. An increasingly secular and scientific world sees apocalypse possibly starting—not over access to markets or nuclear weapons or advanced technologies—but over access to an ancient holy site, the Temple Mount in Jerusalem.

Americans discover that the "End of History" has nothing to do with the triumph of democracy or with America's supposed mission in the world. After saying for centuries, in Theodore Roosevelt's words, that "we stand at Armageddon and we battle for the Lord," we discover that the Lord knew we were battling largely for ourselves and has assigned us no discernable role at all at Armageddon—at least not on His side.

Just at the end of the Cold War, that supposed Armageddon between American capitalism and Russian communism, just when we have won what we saw as the titanic struggle for the future of liberal capitalism, just when Francis Fukuyama proclaims the "End of History," we discover that the battle was largely irrelevant and that the end is just beginning. Control of a 30-acre site in ancient Jerusalem and ownership of a small area on the Jordan's West Bank turn out to be key issues—and not control of West Berlin, Cuba, or the Mekong Delta. We discover that our image of ourselves and our system of government as "the last, best hope of earth" is absurd, if not blasphemous.

Basic principle #2: the Creator is not unjust to draw the final curtain down. Let's remember that we were ready to begin a devastating nuclear exchange if the Soviets attempted to seize West Berlin or to invade Western Europe. When saber-rattling during the Cold War, we were willing to toss around "apocalyptic visions" as threats against Communist bloc leaders—for our own relatively trivial purposes. Who are we to argue that the Creator is unjust to draw history to an end for His much more significant purposes?

Contemporary society could be compared to one of these white supremacist camps in Arkansas or Idaho that have defied the authority of the U.S. government on some specious grounds. It is inevitable that governmental authority will some day be successfully asserted against the white supremacists, most likely during the pursuit of a fugitive from justice. Contemporary society denies and defies the authority of the Creator. His laws are routinely broken. His name is blasphemed regularly. Here, repeatedly, humans made in His image are beaten, tortured, and killed. Here His Son was murdered. Christians have not tried to conceal the fact that some day His authority will be successfully and finally asserted here.

Basic (and most important) principle #3: apocalyptic warnings have always been an essential part of basic Christianity. The world comes with no lifetime warranty, as we who live in a nuclear age should realize. Some regard apocalyptic prophecies as quackery—like the *New Yorker* cartoons showing a long-haired, bearded zealot parading with a sign announcing, "The End is Near." And it is true that an obsession with apocalyptic prophecies has driven some individuals off the deep end. Yet the doctrine of last things, or eschatology, is part of true Christianity, which is a seamless web. The Babe in the manger, the Sermon on the Mount, the social ethic that calls for aid to the homeless, the high standards of personal morality, the Cross and the Second Coming—these are all linked inseparably together.

In his essay "The World's Last Night", C.S. Lewis stated it very clearly:

> Yet is seems to me impossible to retain in any recognizable form our belief in the Divinity of Christ and the truth of the Christian revelation while abandoning, or even persistently neglecting, the promised, and threatened, Return.[1]

Every Sunday, millions of churchgoers around the world recite the Nicene Creed or the Apostles' Creed. The former reads, "And He [Jesus Christ] shall come again with the with glory to judge both the living and the dead, Whose [Christ's] kingdom shall have no end."

Critics often portray apocalyptic talk as motivated by the inner psychological needs of believers. They cannot deal with a changing world so they have devised a way of escape by searching ancient prophecies for predictions of a divine rescue— of them. We can all chuckle over the Millerites of the 1840s, who predicted that the Second Coming would occur on October 22, 1844, prepared themselves for it, and had to sheepishly return to their normal lives, but even then "held to the belief that the millennium was near, however wrong their mathematics."[2]

Now, the New Testament writers occasionally used the certainty of the Second Coming to comfort Christians who were under severe persecution in Nero's Roman Empire. The third chapter of 2 Peter would be one example. Another would be the book of Revelation, which was written during a later period of increased persecution of Christians. A prophecy may have several different purposes, however. The book of Revelation did serve to comfort Christians suffering under the Emperor Domitian's reign, but it would be reductionist to assume that such comfort is its only purpose. Its main purpose goes much deeper than events around 95 A.D.

Similarly, apocalyptic prophecies were not intended to excite the merely escapist curiosity of 20th century American Christians living under relatively comfortable circumstances. The Second Coming is not primarily intended for the rescue of Christians. The skeptics are entirely wrong if they think they are dealing merely with the escapist dreams of a fanatical few.

The Second Coming is the public vindication of Jesus of Nazareth, Son of God and Messiah, and the Apocalypse is the necessary last step in God's plan to bring all things under the authority of Christ:

And he made known to us the mystery of his will according to his good pleasure, which he purposed in Christ, to be put into effect when the times will have reached their fulfilment—to bring all things in heaven and on earth together under one head, even Christ. (Ephesians 1:9–10)

The Apocalyse has a purpose and that is it. Rescuing individual Christians from a world of MTV and Madonna is quite secondary. This public vindication, this Second Coming, is absolutely essential to true Christianity, and is not some secondary doctrine thought up later in order to conveniently get Christians off this toilsome earth and into their eternal rest.

Though believers through the centuries have by faith seen Jesus Christ as resurrected and glorified, the world's last sight of Him was as a condemned criminal dying an excruciating, slow death on a Roman cross.

We are part of Western civilization, which has a tradition of nominal belief in Christianity. We are accustomed to viewing the crucifixion through believers' eyes—at countless Good Friday services and orchestral performances of *The Passion According to St. Matthew* and Handel's *Messiah*. We are accustomed to viewing it as somehow a self-vindicating event. In the eyes of faith, it is a glorious expression of self-denying love.

As a public event, however, the Scriptures make clear that it was a shameful way to die:

"Jesus . . . endured the cross, scorning its shame" (Hebrews 12:2); ". . . the disgrace He bore" (Hebrews 13:13b); "He humbled Himself and became obedient to death—even death on a cross!" (Philippians 2:8b); "Christ redeemed us from the curse of the law by becoming a curse for us, for it is written: 'Cursed is everyone who is hung on a tree'" (Galatians 3:13).

Nothing is more certain than that this Christ will be publicly vindicated and exalted so as to totally reverse this unjust judgment imposed on Him by Pilate, the Roman governor. Christ's Second Coming in power and glory is an essential part of the Christian message. Christ's death on the Cross is not—cannot be—the end of the story.

Instead of longing to be rescued, we Christians ought to eagerly look forward to the time when the Christ Whom we know and love privately (so to speak) will be publicly and gloriously revealed. The prophet Isaiah eloquently describes the contrast between the world's last look at Him and its next look at Him:

> Just as there were many who were appalled at him—his appearance was so disfigured beyond that of any man and his form marred beyond human likeness—so will many nations marvel at him, and kings will shut their mouths because of him. (Isaiah 52:14–15a)[3]

Nothing is more certain than that the Roman execution of Jesus of Nazareth as a common criminal is not the last chapter in His story. Even a common sense notion of what completes a story should tell us that.

What the critics and skeptics ultimately must face is not the whimsical escapism of individual Christians, but the plans of the Almighty God to vindicate His Son and to establish His rule on this earth. They cannot foil His plans. Paradoxically, even their opposition serves to further His plans, for He uses it to bring them to fruition.

Secular opponents of the Gospel think they have successfully confined it to a private world, while their secular, scientific, humanistic views have succeeded in capturing control of the public arena. In *Foolishness to the Greeks*, Lesslie Newbigin makes this distinction between "the public world of what our culture calls facts" and "the private world of beliefs, opinions, and values." He argues that, as a result of the 18th Century Enlightenment, Western societies enthroned the physical and social sciences in the public world of fact, and relegated moral values and divine purposes (thus, Christianity) to a private world of values. Protestant Christianity's response to this challenge "was to accept the dichotomy and withdraw into the private sector." By this acceptance, says Newbigin, "the awesome and winsome claim of Jesus Christ to be alone the Lord of all the world... is effectively silenced."[4]

This is unacceptable and the first step to reversing it, as Newbigin argues, "must be the recovery and firm grasp of a true doctrine of the last things, of eschatology." When the Christ Who has been privately adored comes to publicly reign, that false dichotomy between public facts and private values will be finally ended. That is another reason why the Second Coming is an essential part of true Christianity, not a weird subject of thought among a few fanatics.

Basic principle #4: at heart, Christians are not nostalgic people who long for Wally and the Beaver, Ward and June Cleaver, and the good old 1950s—or for William Jennings Bryan to come back and out-argue Clarence Darrow at the Scopes Trial. We confidently wait for the public vindication and exaltation of our Lord. We look hopefully to the future and repeat the daily prayer of the old Yankee preacher Lyman Beecher in the early 19th century—"Overturn and overturn till He whose right it is shall come and reign, King of nations and King of saints."

Overturn communism, but not in order to bring the blessings of liberal capitalism to the developing world. Overturn the Soviet Union and the Red Army, but not to enable us to say we won the Cold War. Overturn the nuclear arsenals, but not to realize the 1960s hippies' dream world of peace-now, free love, flowers, and cheap drugs. Overturn the two-party dominance of American politics, but not to please Ross Perot. Overturn the political influence of American evangelicals, even, if that is necessary. But overturn, we pray, so that the Man of Sorrows comes to reign as King of Kings and Lord of Lords.

8

OLAF'S VICTORY

A warring Viking since his early youth,
Olaf Haraldsson now conquered for the gentle Nazarene
(And for himself) by sweeping Norway clean
Of Viking gods and heathen idols' groves.
With red beard and piercing, charismatic look,
He (strangely) slew the foes of grace and truth.

The year of our Lord 1030, an awful Wednesday
In July, at Stiklestad by Trondheims Fjord,
Killed in battle, fell Norway's lord,
As ten thousand men collided—with swearing
And with swordplay—nevertheless, through his death
The gospel was preached in Norway.

Near Stiklestad by Trondheims Fjord,
On a cold January day in 1893, another
Olaf came forth from a Norwegian mother—
A 2-pound twin, put in a dresser drawer,
Thought dead, but alive—to age ninety-five.
He came to know St. Olaf's Lord.

His father gone, his grandfather hit by lightning,
To Northern Minnesota in the early days
He came to farm, to log, and finally to praise
His God—though not in battle as his namesake had.
Though Olaf served in World War I,
He never saw Flanders or the fighting.

He served in his living-room easy chair,
Piled high with books, papers and Bible.
Though in his nineties, never idle,
He cared for himself, his vegetable and flower garden,
But more for church, friends and small Minnesota town—
Whom he lifted up in living-room prayer.

Finally, his Norwegian relatives write
To announce a trip, a long-postponed reunion
With Stiklestad's long-lost, near-forgotten son.
On Thursday, in Minnesota's hottest, driest July,
They land after a fourteen-hour flight
But Olaf Hjelde dies that night.

"How much can one 95-year-old man lift?"
The pastor asks us—us!—whose heroes
Are athletes, actors, self-proclaimed "kings"—
Not a praying 95-year-old man,
Whose Norwegian relatives stand
Puzzled—as if from a pagan land—
"Olaf too was washed in the blood of the Lamb"—
And through his death
The gospel is preached to Norway.

(And two weeks later the Easter lilies bloom
Outside the window by the chair in his living room.)

9

HAR DU INTET RUM
FOR JESUS?

Har du intet rum for Jesus,
Ham, som gav sit liv for dig?
Han nu banker på dit hjerte,
Hvisker: sjæl, lad op for mig!

Rum for lysten, rum for verden,
Rum for synd og dårlighed,
Men kun ikke rum for Jesus,
Ham, som døden for dig led.

Har du ingen tid for Jesus,
Ham som dig vil gøre fri?
O. benyt dog nådetiden,
Snart den være kan forbi!

Overgiv dig helt til Jesus,
Lad dig lede ved Hans Ånd,
For dit liv lad Ham kun råde,
Han vil løse syndens band.

Kor:
Rum for Jesus. ærens konge—
O. lad op og byd Ham ind!
Salighed Han med sig bringer.
Ja. Hans herlighed bli'r din!

10

JOURNEY INTO THE INTERIOR OF DENMARK AND NORWAY

Though Scandinavia was my destination, I landed in Amsterdam, since airfare was significantly cheaper to Amsterdam than to any of the Scandinavian capitals.

Amsterdam is the capital of a state of moral anarchy where the trains run on time. The national square of Holland, the Dam, appears to be a continual street festival the "be-ins" held in San Francisco in the 1960s. The Sixties are still going strong in Amsterdam—ironically, on Moses and Aaron Street in front of a citadel of Calvinism, the Nieuwe Kerk. The Dam shows few signs of legalism—whether Mosaic or Calvinist. A grotesque sign advertises an exhibit titled "Torture Instruments Through the Ages"—at a site on Heiligewig (Holy Way) Street.

With its stunning carved wood pulpit, its painted Great Organ and its stained glass windows, the Nieuwe Kerk is currently a museum more than a church. You pay 2 guilders (about $1) for admission. As you enter, you first encounter a sidewalk café, then a shop selling postcards and art books. Tourists saunter through this art museum, as if only the carved and painted details were of interest and not the inner devotion that produced them and that they in turn were meant to encourage.

That is the problem with Amsterdam. The Dutch have preserved the ordered streets and canals and buildings while they have failed to preserve the sense of moral order that produced this outward order. It seems folly to preserve your ancestors' two-by-fours but not their values. You can almost touch the spiritual emptiness at the Dam. Tourists and street people sit in front of the Queen's palace and on the national monument, simply stare at each other and wait for something to happen.

Anne Frank's house is quite the opposite of the Nieuwe Kerk museum. Outwardly, you find little to admire: the house is small, the stairs very narrow and very steep, and the rooms virtually empty of any furniture (the Nazis took most of the families' belongings). Nothing dramatic happened here—except perhaps for the Nazis' raid on the hiding place—and no one comes here to admire that. What you admire is that inner courage, that spiritual resistance to an evil which appeared to have finally triumphed throughout Europe. Still preserved on the wall is a map of Normandy with pins showing the Allied advance toward Holland—an advance too late to save Anne Frank from the death camps.

The train from Amsterdam to Copenhagen went through Germany late at night, which created an atmosphere akin to that of a World War II spy movie. Railroad tracks don't often pass through the newer, postwar sections of cities and many German train stations have a vintage 1940 appearance. The train stopped near the German border as night set in; customs officers speaking German like Max Von Sydow came aboard and demand to see passports; the train moved on through dimly-lit, virtually empty train stations; there were unexpected and unexplained stops and starts; two Swedish women (neutrals) and three Finnish men (allied with Germany) in the compartment slept soundly while this American couldn't sleep a wink all night. The sky was brightening as the ferry boat left Puttgarden, Germany, and headed for beautiful Denmark. After we landed at Rødbyhavn, the Finns seemed amused to observe me looking eagerly out the window at the fields of barley, the cows, and the beech trees. Compared to Finland, the Danish countryside probably seemed quite boring, hardly worthy of the word "scenery." Even the Danish tourism industry is sensitive about this point, it seems, for in Oslo I saw a van advertising vacations in Jutland. The slogan painted on the side read "Danmark—Mere End Du Tror" (Denmark—More Than You Think).

Europe leaves an overwhelming first impression of what can only be called worldliness. People seem very proud of their art and architecture, of their own personal lifestyle, of their status as residents of one of Europe's capitals. Everyone appears a winner in his or her own eyes, but the contestants judge themselves only on external appearances.

No wonder that the Finns appeared somewhat contemptuous of Danish scenery. No wonder that people from Jutland and Funen have often felt that the proud *Københavnere* (residents of Copenhagen) looked down on them. It's undoubtedly true that they do, just as in the United States, city people often look down on rural people: hicks, rubes, rednecks. Pride of place is a great folly. Raised on Hans Christian Andersen's satiric tales of the strutting pride of ducks and balls and other small things, the Danes should best know how foolish it is.

Copenhagen is built like an imperial capital: spacious boulevards, beautiful parks and government buildings in the French Second Empire style. The resulting pride of place is somewhat incongruous, however, because Copenhagen has for 175 years been an imperial capital without much of an empire. In the early 19th century, it was fast becoming a provincial backwater in grave danger of losing its status as a European capital.

Copenhagen's telephone book includes a short, breathless piece praising life in a *verdensby* (world-class city):

> Here you find everything you expect in a large city... a countless number of good, exciting restaurants. Galleries and cafes. Theaters, museums, cinemas. Tivoli.... And every day something is happening.... Premieres, art exhibitions, concerts and spontaneous entertainment and self-expression.... Music, colors, ambience. You go people-watching. Meet your friends. Have fun.[1]

My first Sunday in Copenhagen, I strolled down Strøget, the famous pedestrian shopping street, with its crowds of window-gazers, people-watchers, exhibitionists, tourists and thrill-seekers seeking the "music, colors, ambience." Viewed from a spiritual perspective, the ambience seemed tragic, not exciting. Something was happening, but something out of *Pilgrims Progress* more than a city promoter's paean of praise. The literal translation of *verdensby* would be "the world's city" (not God's city) and this *verdensby* seemed like Vanity Fair as John Bunyan described it:

> They contrived here to set up a fair; a fair wherein should be sold all sorts of vanity, and that it should last all the year long. Therefore at this fair are all such merchandise sold... and delights of all sorts.... And, moreover, at this fair there is at all times to be seen jugglings, cheats, games, plays, fools, apes, knaves, and rogues, and that of every kind. Here are to be seen, too, and that for nothing, thefts, murders, false swearers, and that of a blood-red color.

That description sounds harsh and puritanical to our modern ears. No doubt some socially redeeming value could be found for most of the merchandise and entertainments along Strøget. Buyan's point was not that all the amusements were evil, but that they distracted pilgrims from the very real delights of the Celestial City. Not a killjoy angered to see anyone having fun, Bunyan was a Christian angered to see others cheated of eternal life by a few baubles and beads.

Over in Vor Frue Kirke (Church of Our Lady), a hymn in the hymnal spoke of the real delights of the spiritual life:

> The Spirit is better than flesh and blood;
> The Lord is kind-hearted and delicious. (!)
> Christians see joyous days.[2]

DANISH CHRISTIANS WITNESS IN COPENHAGEN

That Sunday I attended services a Kristuskirken (Christ Church), a Danish Baptist church in the Nørrebro section of Copenhagen. A Southern Baptist minister from Greenville, South Carolina, conducted the English-language service in a rich Southern accent. After the English service, he hosted a coffee hour, and I had the opportunity to meet the American Consul, who was a former Minnesotan, and a student from Gustavus Adolphus College in St. Peter, Minnesota.

After the Danish-language service, the Danes served coffee in "Café nr.9," an alternative café operated by some young members of Kristuskirken as an effort at "friendship evangelization." There I tried out my halting Danish on a young woman who worked for *Berlingske Tidende*, the more conservative newspaper in Copenhagen. It was a mistake to 33 1/3 r.p.m. Danish to her. She just answered back in 78 r.p.m. Danish. Better to talk English if all you know how to hear is English.

I felt encouraged to see firsthand a vibrant Christian movement in Denmark, since I had heard only about the average Dane's lack of interest in Christianity. A Christian political party, the Kristeligt Folkeparti (Christian People's Party) manages to elect some representatives to the Folketing (Parliament). During a short visit, I found it difficult to discover exactly what the Kristeligt Folkeparti supports or opposes. My favourable opinion of it may be uninformed. Certainly, as the Consul explained, the Danish multi-party system with its eight political parties and proportional representation is chaotic.

Still, the principle seems sound. If the primary Christian goal in politics, as in every other field, is to present a true and balanced witness for Christ and not necessarily to win elections, then a separate Christian party is desirable. It limits the political compromises which distort that witness. In the United States, many evangelical Christians have compromised with the materialistic, Wall Street wing of the Republican party. The resulting coalition seriously compromises the anti-materialistic message of Jesus Christ, though it has won a few presidential elections.

While participating in politics, Christians ought to not create any unnecessary divisions within the Body of Christ over political issues. Currently our two-party system unnecessarily polarizes American evangelicals. Republicans advocate economic freedom for entrepreneurs to operate apart from much sense of responsibility for the poor. Democrats advocate cultural and social freedom for individuals to act apart from Judeo-Christian concepts of personal morality.

Each party correctly accuses the other of indifference to the consequences. Democrats accuse Republicans of being indifferent to the grossly unequal distributions of wealth and income. Republicans accuse Democrats of indifference to the high abortion rate, pornography, drug abuse, and decline of the family which results from moral relativism. These accusations divide Christians into two camps: those concerned with "social issues" and those concerned about social and economic justice. Of course, the Lord Jesus Christ is concerned about both, and indifferent to neither poverty nor immorality. The two rival political camps perpetuate this false dichotomy.

Perhaps an American "Christian People's Party" could help to heal this division, erase this false dichotomy, and present a united Christian witness.

Kristeligt Dagblad (Christian Daily) provides Christians with complete daily coverage of domestic and foreign news, church news, cultural events, and education. I felt encouraged to see on the newspaper's masthead this motto: "Ikke ved magt og ikke ved styrke, men ved min Ånd, siger Hærskarers Herre" (Not by power and not by strength, but by My spirit, says the Lord of Hosts). A weekly paper called *Udfordringen* (The Challenge) is more evangelistic in subject matter and in style. Denmark's secularisation has forced Christians to develop their own party, their own newspapers and their own institutions. Though secularisation may be undesirable, this consequence seems desirable.

OLSOK (ST. OLAF'S) WEEK IN NORWAY

From Copenhagen, my wife and I took a weekend trip to the Trondheim area of Norway to visit relatives of her grandfather, Olaf Hjelde.

Viewed retrospectively from a railroad car hurtling through a narrow gorge beneath Norway's towering, still snow-clad mountains, Copenhagen appeared even more a *snævre* little city dedicated to man's desire to immortalize himself. The light green of weathered copper seems the city's symbol—seen in the green copper spires and towers and in the green copper-coated statues of kings on horseback, famous writers, long-forgotten statesmen, and naked goddesses. Is this faded-green immortality worth it—with a pigeon on your head, a black streak running down your left cheek and graffiti painted across your name?

Norway's heights are Creator-made and much more spectacular. There are few statues. Along Lake Mjosa, the farms gingerly climb the steep slope up from the water. Tractors perform a balancing act to stay upright while cutting hay on the steep hillsides. The oats are ripening from blue-green to yellow. On the mountaintop, clouds cast shadows on dark green forests and make them darker still, while the sun reflects off the yellow oats halfway down to the lake, and a white wooden church glistens by the water.

Farther up the Gudbrandsdalen, a narrow river with churning white rapids hurtles past on its way to Lake Mjosa. In certain places this river valley has no floor—just walls which the railroad track barely clings to or tunnels through. Seeking secure footing, the track crosses from one side of the river to the other and back again.

At Dovre, the sunlight reflected off the snow on some distant mountains. Then we came out onto a high plateau. We saw no farms, just bare rock, scrub trees, moss or lichen on the ground, and snow fences to protect the track from drifting snow. Now we were past the watershed divide, and the rivers started flowing west to Trondheims Fjord. The descent seemed steeper than the ascent up to the divide. We came down the ancient invasions path into the Trøndelag, into the interior of Norway.

With only four hours to spend in Trondheim, we walked up to Nidaros Domkirke (Cathedral), built in the 12th and 13th centuries on the site of St. Olaf's grave. A spectacular example of Gothic church architecture, this church was renowned as a holy destination for religious pilgrims in the late Middle Ages. Just as we arrived at the cathedral, hundreds of men in black tuxedos and women in evening dresses were filling in for a special worship service sponsored by the Good Templars. It was "Olsok" week, a week of special events honouring Norway's "eternal" king, St. Olaf, and his death at Stiklestad battlefield on July 29, 1030 A.D. We sneaked into the Domkirke after the tuxedos were seated. Hundreds of worshippers filled the cathedral.

Appropriately, the first hymn sung by choir and congregation was N.F.S. Grundtvig's "Kirken denne er et gammelt hus" ("Built On a Rock The Church Doth Stand" is the English version). As the music and the Word resounded beneath the high, vaulted ceiling, it felt as if a thousand years of Christianity in Norway were being focused on one spot, the way a magnifying glass focuses the sun's rays until the dry grass can stand it no longer and bursts into flame. It felt as if we had reached the interior of Norwegian Christianity. Lit by the living faith of at least some of these hundreds of Norwegians, Nidaros Domkirke was a sharp contrast to the museum-like death of the Nieuwe Kerk in Amsterdam.

From Trondheim, we continued by train north to the Stiklestad area of North Trøndelag, where my wife's relatives lived. Without having planned it, we arrived on the very weekend of Olsok festivities at Siklestad, which included the outdoor play about King Olaf, and a special concert in the 11th century Stiklestad church built on the spot where King Olaf was said to have died.

Olaf Haraldsson began his career as a Viking. He was baptized in Normandy when about 18 years old. Three years later, Olaf advanced into the Trøndelag to win the kingship of Norway. He probably took the same invasion path our train followed. As king, he firmly established institutionalized

Christianity in Norway, sometimes by harsh means such as executing, blinding, maiming or evicting reluctant pagans. No doubt baptism seemed preferable to many. He used Viking means to accomplish ostensibly Christian ends, but "by the time he died Norway was a Christian country, and no relapse into heathendom was possible," according to one historian.[3]

After being deposed as king, Olaf sought refuge in Russia, only to return in 1030 to reclaim his throne. Outnumbered perhaps four-to-one, his ragtag army was soundly beaten at Stiklestad and Olaf was slain. Legend completes the story. Supposedly, he died on his birthday; a solar eclipse occurred during the battle; even his enemies were healed by touching blood from his corpse; prayers to St. Olaf were answered; and, his body didn't decay—even hair and beard grew in the grave (!). In death, Olaf won his place as Norway's "eternal King."

Though we hardly believed all the legends, we were pleasantly surprised to find ourselves in Stiklestad during Olsok week. A month had passed since midsummer's eve, yet the sky still seemed at perpetual twilight when our hosts walked us all around the Stiklestad site at midnight. They seemed embarrassed as they encountered a drunken enemy or aquaintance—knowing no Norwegian, we were hard-pressed to tell which—who stumbled on the outskirts of the crowd.

On this Friday night, "Dollie de Luxe," a Norwegian female rock-opera group, was performing "Which Witch," a *hekseoperaen* (witch opera) on the outdoor stage at Siklestad. Ironically, members of King Olaf's army, who would march for Christianity during Sunday's performance, were hired to maintain order in case of crowd unruliness during the "witch opera."

Some 9,000 people attended the next day's staging of the "Spelet om Heilag Olav" (The Play About St. Olaf). The St. Olaf play contrasts the old pagan ways on Sun Dances, spells and superstitions with the Christianity promoted by King Olaf. Though the actor playing the Christian King gave a strong performance, the times have subtly altered the play so that the pagan characters seem stronger, the pagan ways seem not the old but the new ways, the high-collared bishops and choir boys seem outdated and too formal, while the pagan youths cavorting licentiously on the hillside closely resemble the street youths of Amsterdam or Copenhagen of Oslo. One of the old pagan customs which King Olaf denounces in the play is the custom of abandoning unwanted babies in the woods. Abortion is legal in both Norway and Denmark. The battle of Stiklestad is far from being over.

While King Olaf's sainthood can perhaps be doubted—he was mostly motivated by a desire to unite Norway under *his* rule—he did consolidate and establish Christianity in Norway. Norway and much of Europe seems to have grown tired of Christianity. Reporting on Olsok week in Stiklestad, the newspaper *Adresseavisen* featured a photo of a stunning blonde from Dollie de Luxe, and two stories about "Which Witch," and gave little space to the long-familiar St. Olaf play, which the reporter termed "quite banal."

ALIENS AND STRANGERS

From Stiklestad, we travelled back to Oslo. My wife caught a flight back to Minnesota, while I caught a train for Kristiansand, a boat for Denmark, and the DSB train to Brønderslev, where I intended to stay for my remaining four weeks in Denmark.

Brønderslev is a small city of 8,000 located about 15 miles north of Aalborg in Vendsyssel, an area of northern Jutland. One Copenhagen resident offered some disparaging remarks about the place and its people when he heard I was headed for Vendsyssel. He led me to believe that it did not rank at the very top of the Danish hierarchy of places. Brønderslev is a modern, clean, new city, a railroad town (*stationsby*) dating from the late 19th century. It thus lacks the ancient features of some Danish towns.

Imitating the capital like provincial cities everywhere, it has its modest *gågade* (pedestrian street) downtown, but few world class travellers stroll there. Teenagers hang out there late at night. On the "motorized" streets, scooters and motorbikes take youths to the local equivalent of a Dairy Queen.

The youth hostel was full, so they directed me to a private home for lodging. An elderly couple—Baptists, it turned out—rented me a room in their basement for 70 *kroner* a night. Though they had relatives in Minnesota, they spoke no English or else were reluctant to try out their English. We communicated in Danish. Once they discovered that I had connections to some Baptists in Vendsyssel, they invited me up every morning to have breakfast with them.

Several other families invited me into their homes. At one home, the young son was watching the Cubs play the Mets. At the Baptist minister's home, his teenage daughters and a friend were watching "thirtysomething" complete with Danish subtitles. How much can they really understand about the crisis of the aging among American Baby-Boomers? The age difference, the language barrier and the cultural gap would all seem to lessen the chances for understanding. Late one Sunday night, the minister turned on a televised Danish soccer game. When we were up in the Trøndelag, we sat with relatives watching two northern Norwegian teams play Sunday night soccer.

When in a foreign country, sporting events often seem devoid of meaning or interest. What interest could we possibly have in a Sunday night soccer game between Tromsø and Molde? Could we sit on the edge of our seats for fear that the Molde would lose? We necessarily lacked the context of the contest. Was Tromsø the underdog, the poor northern town, fighting the rich "city slickers" from southern Molde? Or had Tromsø been hated for years for hiring professional Swedes to defeat the good Norwegians who played for the other cities' teams? What was the story here?

In American sports, the announcers set up the story when they do the five-minute introductory segment. In this game, we will see if Joe Schmidt can come back after knee surgery, or if the Sox can maintain their five-game winning streak without their star third-basemen. To the foreign tourist in America, none of this would make much sense or seem that important if it did.

The tourist in a foreign country can see sporting events for what they are—mere amusements, mere trifles. In his or her own land, the native sees them for what they can never be—trials of strength to prove his city's or his own worth. He or she anguishes over the home team's fate, gets a splitting headache from anxiety during a Super Bowl game, and suffers from post-game depression or euphoria.

Traveling abroad for long periods can be like a church retreat, where you are forced out of the world for a time ("What NOT to bring—Portable stereo, TV, alcohol, tobacco or drugs. NO EXCEPTIONS!"). Abroad, you are very much in the world, but can't understand much of it due to language and cultural differences. And, after a week or two you realize that not everything foreign is important. The rivalry between Tromsø and Molde is not important: your time here is short, and once back in the United States, both will be forgotten. You feel partially dead to the world around you. It is like returning home late Sunday night from a church retreat, casually picking up the Sunday newspaper and glancing at stories that now seem trivial in light of the spiritual experiences of the weekend. You have nearly forgotten the context.

While spending Sundays at the Baptist minister's home, I soon felt less interested in the Sunday newspaper. The pastor's copy of John Stott's book, *The Cross of Christ*, caught my attention instead. I read it for hours, on a beautiful day in Denmark with its *dejlig* (beautiful) countryside and myself with only a few precious weeks to enjoy it. And, really, it is the cross of Christ that most powerfully makes us dead to the world. Paul writes,

> May I never boast except in the cross of our Lord Jesus Christ, through which the world has been crucified to me, and I to the world. (Galatians 6:14)

The cross makes amusements and entertainments seem trivial, even if we know the context and the story. The cross makes our stay here seem temporary. The picture of this world's permanent residents nailing the Son of God to the cross makes us feel that we must be tourists, that we are "aliens and strangers in the world" (1 Peter 2:11a).[4]

Traveling in a foreign land makes you feel like an alien and a stranger. *Item.* You board the front car in a train only to be told that you cannot sit there, so you retreat to the rear cars (but leave your briefcase in the front car). Unbeknownst to you, the train is divided and the front car is sent to a different city.

Item. You arrive in a strange city in the rain. Surprisingly, there is no place to store your suitcase, so you hide it behind some bushes so you can walk around the city to find lodging. Then you haul it to the hotel.

Item. You travel across the country to find materials stored at one library, only to find that when you arrive at 1 PM that the library closes at 2 PM—and that you must request the materials one day in advance.

Item. At the supermarket checkout counter, you pay for the groceries and wait for the clerk to bag them only to have a cold stare tell you that here clerks do not bag groceries—customers do.

Things happen that convince you that life here was not designed with you in mind.

We are reluctant to admit these truths when on our home turf. We delude ourselves into believing that lifelong residence means we belong. Athletic teams contribute to this myth. We all cheer for the Twins, Vikings, North Stars and Gophers. The Regional section of the bookstore fosters other myths: all Minnesotans are understated Scandinavians who talk alike, love to cook with wild rice, enjoy ethnic jokes, and go up to the lake on weekends. Myths foster a sense of belonging.

But the cross of Christ creates a sense that we do not belong. The travelling Christian can rediscover that "alien and stranger" status, and can accept it as natural and desirable, something to continue when he or she returns "home":

> And they admitted that they were aliens and strangers on earth. People who say such things show that they are looking for a country of their own. If they had been thinking of the country they had left, they would have had opportunity to return. Instead, they were longing for a better country—a heavenly one. Therefore God is not ashamed to be called their God, for he has prepared a city for them. (Hebrews 11:13b–16)

DANISH COUNTRYSIDE AND CHRISTIANITY

There is nothing like the Danish countryside to reassure you that there will always be a bountiful harvest.

It was harvest time in Denmark. They had an early spring and a hot June, so the dusty, dark-yellow fields of wheat, barley and oats were definitely ready to harvest. Coming back to Brønderslev from Thisted, I counted 34 combines out harvesting. On the weekend, children were out helping their fathers with the harvest—romping among straw bales or riding in the tractor cab or standing in the wagon to evenly distribute the constantly-flowing stream of fresh grain.

Almost all Danish houses are built of brick. Lumber for construction is in short supply. Some are built of a dark, off-yellow brick that seems the exact same color as the ripe barley fields ready for harvest. And, their dark, nearly black, roofs seem the same color as the newly-plowed fields already harvested. Denmark appears color-coordinated.

The Danish countryside is so neat and clean that when you walk along and smell manure, you half imagine the smell comes from *you*, for you can't see any other obvious source.

The Danish countryside is like a poem. Everything superfluous is left out. The Danes are parsimonious with their space. It is in short supply and is seldom wasted. The country roads are narrow and their shoulders almost non-existent. Barley and oats are planted right up to the road itself. There is no ditch. You can almost reach out and touch the crops as you walk by.

The Danish countryside which those Finns regarded as boring has a way of surprising you. Walking out of town, you pass by the barley or wheat fields of an ordinary farm, then come to a hill with a fine view of what appears to be sheep grazing on the slope across the valley, but as you come closer they turn out to be chalk-white cows. In the valley is a manor house, several hundred years old and surrounded by a moat. Coming up out of the valley, a shaded country lane takes you into a very dark forest, but a highway comes along and takes you back to ordinary barley fields and so into town again. And, you have only travelled three miles!

If anything, though, Denmark has too much of a peaceful, comfortable appearance, which doesn't always accurately reflect reality. Danes are concerned about the widespread public drunkenness and the high level of alcoholism. Copenhagen's park workers have refused to clean parks in the Vesterbro neighborhood, because some have cut themselves on the many needles discarded by drug addicts. They fear contact with needles contaminated by the AIDS virus.

Some Danish youth rebel against the comfortableness and middle-class stability of Denmark. At an art exhibition at Charlottenborg in Copenhagen, someone had scrawled the message, "Down with Bourgeois Art." The exhibition itself displayed real proletarian art (supposedly) and some of it was definitely obscene. My guide, an older woman from the upper middle class, took a look around with some disgust and decided to leave. Did she know what was really wrong with this art or was it simply a question of good taste?

The respectable middle and upper class Danes do not seem to know what to make of the punk youth on the streets of their Copenhagen or their Aalborg. For people who have neatly codified good and evil into laws of outward style, good taste and respectability, such an outward rebellion with its atrocious mixture of hair colors is unexplainable and astonishing.

Do Danish youth equate Christianity with middle class respectability? Many of their parents seem to have turned it into that—if they still profess it at all. Unfortunately, in Denmark infant baptism (the vast majority of Danes are baptized as infants) seems to have worked more like a childhood inoculation, a sort of DPT shot guaranteeing that the Child will not catch Christianity for the rest of his or her life. Danish philosopher Søren Kierkegaard's criticism of the state church *(folkekirken)* seems well-taken. The goal of the state church is to create as many "Christians" as possible,

> And that is very easily done ... get a hold of the children, then give each child a drop of water on the head—then he is a Christian— then in a very short time we have more Christians than there are herring during the herring season, Christians by the millions.[5]

One result is church attendance not at all reminiscent of schools of herring. According to one article in *Berlingske Tidende*, it is not uncommon to see only a half-dozen to two dozen churchgoers at a large Copenhagen church on a Sunday morning. The auther, who was the president of a congregation in suburban Copenhagen, reported that the parents of teenage youth don't attend church while "the teenagers themselves attend church for the last time at confirmation and never show up again."[6]

While I was in Denmark, another writer wrote a piece in *Berlingske Tidende* arguing that many Danes would attend church to hear the beautiful church music if only they were not thereby faced with the necessity of reciting the Creed, which they no longer believe!

Do such parents care about their children's spiritual condition? So long as the boy or girl does nothing outwardly outrageous, such as wearing a pierced lip-ring or a Mohawk hair style, they would seem to have no basis for praising or condemning youths choices. In a society stressing outward appearances, the worst sins are in matters of personal appearance. Youth must see through such hypocrisy.

Of course, this problem is not confined to Denmark, but appears throughout the liberal, capitalist West. A *Weekendavisen* editorial ("Tomhedens sejr"—the victory of emptiness) commenting on Francis Fukuyama's piece, "The End of History," pointed to a major reason why materialistic, democratic, capitalist societies have difficulty giving a clear sense of direction to youth. A certain emptiness lies at the heart of such societies. Freedom itself cannot guide the young into an understanding of what is truly important and why.[7]

When we were in Norway, we stayed with a very friendly middle class family. On their living room wall they had a beautiful picture featuring the words and music to a song honoring *Bydel Otte* (City Section 8). The numerous small suburbs of Oslo, each with its own name and its own history, have been artificially united into numbered city sections. This song attempted to cultivate warm, sentimental feelings for *Bydel Otte*. I developed a real fondness for this family of four, but left wondering whether the teen-age children would long remain loyal to middle-class respectability, *Bydel Otte*, a nice 9-to-5 job, and a good stamp collection. Won't they discover deeper spiritual needs that can't be satisfied by some city planner's concept of quality urban living?

When I was a city clerk, and a business in that small town failed or looked like it might fail, I would half-humorously think of the verse from Hebrews that describes Abraham's faith: "For he was looking forward to the city with foundations" (Hebrews 11:10). I hope these Oslo teenagers develop warm feelings for that city "whose architect and builder is God," rather than for *Bydel Otte*.

There was a humorous definition in one of the Copenhagen newspapers: a Lutheran is a soul with two ears. That is a good example of Danish understated humor, that works by radically oversimplifying things. Yet the definition also strips away many of the little knick-knacks of life and reveals a serious truth: we are all of us just souls with two ears. May these Oslo youths, and Danish youths, seriously listen to the Word that can save their souls. As our Lord said, "If anyone has ears to hear, let him hear" (Mark 4:23).

May we American evangelicals truly hear the lessons of Europe, of once solidly Christian countries now apathetic under the weight of their own cultural history, bored of their oft-repeated litany of Christian philosophers, tired of the roll call of Christian heroes such as Calvin, Luther, Grundtvig and Kierkegaard. There is a subtle process whereby a movement turns in upon itself and begins to study its own past and analyze its own internal workings and loses its vision of the crucified Christ. Evangelicalism can become merely a set of cultural artifacts: the Sandi Patti School of Music, the collected works of Carl F. H. Henry, a doctoral dissertation on "The Harvard Fundamentalists and Billy Graham's 1957 New York City Crusade: A Study in Alternative Evangelical Discourses."

We are only souls with two ears apiece. Only the love of the crucified Christ can really speak to our souls and to the souls of those who hear us. Time is limited and we must practice an economy of words, as the Danish countryside shows an economy of space. What is inessential must be left out. What is essential is Christ crucified, risen and coming again.

11

JEREMIAD

"You'll be thinkin' you'll be President too,"
Muttered the Irish gardener to young Henry,
The truant marched to school
By a quiet President-grandfather,
The boy charging across Boston Common
In the schoolboys' snowball battle,
The young man in Civil War London.

The Constitution, his family's heirloom,
The White House, his family's dwelling.
Himself, a chronicler of presidents, the nation,
And other failures: Jefferson, Gallatin,
John Randolph, his own education.
His faith in moral principles, abandoned.
His charming wife, a suicide.

Tears run down my cheeks at the
Destruction of the daughter of my people.

In rainy New Salem in just-budded April,
Young America sits on the log store's porch,

Bites an apple, reads a law book, and dreams.
From the log motel's porch, though,
Impending crisis and Civil War loom—it seems
Constitution and politicians must agree
to plead nolo contendere.

Tears run down my cheeks at the
Destruction of the dreams of my people.
August 1974, somewhere east of Cleveland,
The Greyhound driver's portable TV
Announces the resignation—Hail to the Chief!—
Then that eerie weekend in Washington,
Limousines driving through the White House gates
While the People's Bicentennial Commission debates
Whether to renounce the use of violence.

April 1975, through rainy Boston,
Along streets and country lanes
Wet asphalt glistens between stone walls.
Lexington at midnight, cars cruising,
Like a college town celebrating homecoming—
No fasting, no sermon, no prayers said—
And terrible failures lie ahead.

Concord's crowded with Bicentennial
Sightseers sleeping on unscreened porches,
Yet there's a perch on the North Bridge railing.
The President's motorcade, sirens wailing.
National Guard jeeps, the helicopter overhead,
Looking for assassins behind stone walls.
The President races like a redcoat back to Boston.

Tears run down my cheeks at the
Destruction of the chief of my people.

A South Dakota boy goes forward
During the small-town Methodist revival,
Then at the 1948 convention—into the sunshine
He leads liberals, and the self-interest groups,
Each sends a spokesperson out in the sub-zero cold,
As Congress is bused in for the funeral
While Billy Graham walks away alone.

Tears ran down my cheeks at the
Death of the Happy Warrior.

Tall debts sailing home into New York Harbor;
The nation's been twelve years at sea
Chasing will-o-the-wisps,
Hearing flattery, speaking lies,
Returning empty-handed to bankruptcy
Giving itself a hero's welcome,
A ticker-tape parade—the hero buys.

October 1, 1990, east of Grand Forks,
At midnight, the government on death row,
The car radio picks up a Denver talk show
Host asking listeners if they believe in a reprieve,
If they hate to see a government shut down.
No, they'll do just fine on their own.
What does a consumer need a country for?

"You'll be thinkin' you'll be President too,"
They're telling a Texas billionaire,
Talk show guest, and phone-in friend.
The consumer needs an owner-manager
Who'll keep the prices low, the help friendly—
"Good morning, welcome to your country"—
But the hands-on owner sells out in the end.

Tears run down my cheeks at the
Destruction of the daughter of my people.

12

SETTING ASIDE GOD'S COMMANDS TO OBSERVE TRADITIONS

When returning from an overseas trip of several weeks, this American felt strongly relieved to be back in the United States. Part of that feeling is homesickness for the sights, the language, and the culture of one's childhood. Part is a longing to see family and friends again. Part may be because a trip to Europe has revealed that certain aspects of American life are to be preferred over European customs. Homecoming brings out those feelings of love of country. However, we must carefully distinguish what in our country is worthy of love, and what might not be.

We should love America and be grateful to this country because the gospel of Jesus Christ has for centuries been more freely preached, more fully accepted, and perhaps more widely practiced here than in almost any other country in the world—with only a few possible exceptions. But we must beware of any patriotism which, like a Trojan horse, brings hidden within itself a false gospel which is at odds with Christ's gospel.

Historians Richard Pierard and Robert Linder have stated clearly the difference between our public faith of Americanism and true Christianity: "the public faith's deistic unitarianism ignores the scandal of the cross and the particularity of the religion which insists that God has shown humanity his face in Jesus Christ." At inaugurations and prayer breakfasts, they report, "it was permissible to talk about God in general but not Jesus Christ in particular."[1]

Many nations do not create a public faith that differs from Christianity. Consider Norway's King Olav, who when visiting a church in Copenhagen expressed the hope that "this church could be a blessing until Jesus comes again."[2] (!) Can we imagine an American president referring so openly to Jesus Christ and not being severely criticized for denying the public faith?

How did this public faith develop and how has it spread throughout American culture?

THE FALSE GOSPEL OF AMERICANISM

From the very beginning of American history, thinkers and dreamers have made strong and persuasive attempts to create a false gospel of Americanism with strong similarities to the Christian gospel: repentance from sin, a new birth, a new chosen people, a new promised land, and a mission to save the world and bring in a new era of righteousness.

Long before the settlement of what is now the United States, some Europeans were indulging in the hope that in a New World (instead of in a new commitment to the old gospel) they could find deliverance from the burden of Europe's problems. They realized that it would be exceedingly difficult to obey the simple Christian gospel in order to reform a society that had complicated its existence with a bewildering array of customs, class differences, and political traditions. So they dreamed of bypassing the problem by finding a New World (instead of a new birth) where they could start afresh. As historian Michael Kammen wrote in *People of Paradox*:

> the idea of America, as El Dorado and Paradise, surfaced before the fact of America, prior to colonization . . . . Sir Thomas More's *Utopia*, for example, preceded by more than a century the utopian schemes of Puritan Boston or Pilgrim Plymouth.

Supposedly an account of a new land discovered by a Portuguese adventurer who had accompanied Americgo Vespucci on a voyage to the New World, More's *Utopia* contrasted old, corrupt Europe and a new promised land. The sins to be repented of were Europe's sins: militarism, luxury, diplomatic deception, extremes of wealth and poverty, and tyrannical rulers. These sins did not characterize the new world of Utopia, where peace, simplicity, honesty, equality and democracy ruled. (Utopia means "nowhere.")

Sir Thomas More described the Utopians' religious beliefs in words that sound oddly prophetic in light of the current religious pluralism in American society:

> Some worship the sun as a god, others the moon,
> and still others some one of the planets. Others worship some
> man pre-eminent in virtue or glory,
> not only as a god, but as the supreme god.[3]

They practiced tolerance towards all such beliefs, even towards the Christianity which the explorers brought. They punished only one Utopian convert to Christianity, one "newly baptized convert" who "condemned all other rites as profane and loudly denounced their celebrants as wicked and impious men fit for hell fire." Religious toleration accompanied by the rule of reason was the Utopians' chief virtue in spiritual matters.

Those Europeans who actually moved to the New World so glowingly fictionalized by More supposedly experienced a new birth. Perhaps the best-known expression of this idea is found in Hector St. John de Crevecoeur's non-fictional *Letters from an American Farmer* (1782):

> What then is the American, this new man? He is an American, who leaving behind him all his ancient prejudices and manners, receives new ones from the new mode of life he has embraced, the new government he obeys, and the new rank he holds . . . . Here individuals of all nations are melted into a new race of men, whose labours and posterity will one day cause great changes in the world.[4]

Having repented of his ancient prejudices, the European received a new life—and was formed along with other ex-Europeans into a "new race of men," who had a near-messianic task of producing "great changes in the world."

From the idea of "this new man," thinkers made the easy leap to the idea that Americans were a new chosen people with the mission of bringing liberty and democracy to the nations. The French stateman Turgot exclaimed, "This people is the hope of the human race. It may become the model."[5] Abraham Lincoln expressed the idea most strongly when he called America "the last, best hope of earth."

Historians Pierard and Linder have outlined some elements in this "civil religion": the idea that America is a chosen nation, the millenial hopes attached to that chosen nation, the great "prophets" such as Washington, Jefferson, and Lincoln leading the nation to the fulfillment of those hopes, the near worship of the flag.

Americans feel a false sense of security in this false gospel that feels comfortingly like Christianity—complete with repentance, a new birth, "chosen people" status, and a mission. The pioneers' westward movement continually renewed the delusion that what Americans needed was not a new birth but a new place.

Yet this false gospel simply doesn't deliver people—either from personal sins or from social injustices—and it never did. It doesn't deliver from divorce, from teen suicide, from drug and alcohol dependency, from inner-city poverty or from crime. Pointing that out is not anti-American. Every other nation has most of those same problems, and Norwegian-ness, German-ness, or French-ness are equally unable to deliver people from them.

Since this is America, we must examine Americanism, which is not Christianity, but a false gospel. What are the consequences of this false gospel in our national life, both today and in the past?

THE FALSE THEOLOGY OF THE FOUNDERS: REPUBLICANISM

The first consequence was that when this New World settlement achieved its political independence, the utopian, non-Christian hopes placed on its discovery and settlement were transfered to its political birth. Just as Europeans placed a messianic meaning upon the initial settling of the New World, so Americans (and some Europeans) also placed a messianic meaning upon the American Revolution and the following period of constitution-making. The nation was politically "born" with a false theology of republicanism that promised more than it could ever deliver.

What was new in the 1770s and 1780s was not the discovery of a continent but the rediscovery and reapplication of an old ideology, republicanism. The historian Gordon S. Wood reminds us: "republicanism was in every way a radical ideology—as radical for the eighteenth century as Marxism was to be for the nineteenth century."[6] Though not as openly hostile to

81

Christianity as Marxism, it subtly undermined the Christian view of God and man.

Derived from the political ideas of the pagan republics of ancient Greece and Rome, republicanism stressed the common good, the well-being of the society and the state, not the worship of God and the salvation of individual souls. It defined virtue as the duty of the citizen to sacrifice private interests for the public good, not as obedience to God's commands. Selfishness and self-indulgence were vices, not because they were contrary to God's commands, but because they were contrary to the good of the commonwealth. Bible-reading and prayer were not necessary for maintaining virtue; economic independence and property-ownership would create and preserve it. Hence, the independent, property-owning farmers were, in Jefferson's words, "the chosen people of God, if ever he had a chosen people."

Why did many Americans who had been taught Christian truths by devoutly Christian parents accept a philosophy that subtly turned Christianity on its head? That question raises issues too numerous to resolve in this essay; however, I would suggest that the wealthy, politically-ambitious, cultured gentry increasingly found unacceptable Christianity's call for humility, self-denial, obedience to authority, unlimited charity towards the poor, rigorous personal morality, and self-sacrificing love towards God. The gentry leaders of the Revolutionary era pictured themselves as Empire-builders and Law-givers who would win immortality and posterity's undying gratitude. The gospel of the crucified Nazarene simply did not encourage these inflated ambitions. It positively discouraged them. However, unlike later Marxists, these gentry leaders were not eager to cast aside the morality, the respect for tradition, and the social stability which they associated with Christianity. In republicanism, they hoped to find a philosophy which preserved the benefits of Christianity while freeing them and their nation from its constraints so that they could fulfill their ambitions.

Republicanism offered a hard, realistic view of humanity. Not soft or sentimental, it stressed human depravity, the inevitability of human failure, and the need for eternal vigilance against corruption and tyranny. That sounded comfortingly like Christianity. Republicanism offered a return to first principles, though to the principles of the ancient Roman republic and not to those of the first-century Christian church. It respected tradition and the ancients. It was conservative in that sense, and accorded with Christianity's respect for the past.

That partially explains republicanism's appeal to Revolutionary era leaders. Why did it appeal to common, ordinary Americans who had no ambitions for fame and a Founder's immortal name? Again, the question is too complicated to answer satisfactorily. Perhaps part of the answer is republicanism's glorification of the ordinary citizens—the farmers who were the "chosen people of God." They may have been flattered to hear that the fate of the nation depended on their virtue. Also, republicanism promised the citizen personal independence and equality, both of which were very attractive in an age of economic dependence and deference to the higher classes.

THE FALSE MORALITY OF CONSTITUTIONALISM

"And why do you break the command of God for the sake of your tradition?" (Matthew 15:3)

The second consequence was that the founding documents of the American nation—the Constitution and the Declaration—

came to be invested with a mystical, almost religious significance. According to Pierard and Linder, they "became the sacred scriptures of the new public faith." The messianic meaning, which had been attached to the idea of America, was conveyed to the documents that formally created the nation. That was understandable, given the importance which American republicanism placed on written constitutions: "these public documents became the covenants which bound the people of the nation together in a political and religious union." The Constitution became a political substitute for Scripture. The nation looked to the Constitution for the basic principles of its political existence, and sought to interpret its phrases rightly in order to preserve liberty and order.

Throughout our history we have been tempted to substitute these mere legal documents for God's commands. Instead of asking whether something was right or wrong in light of God's revelation, we have conducted much of our public debate in terms of peripheral questions of constitutionality. We have hypocritically used constitutionalism to sanction gross wrongdoing.

Before the Civil War, Southerners hid behind the argument that the Constitution directly or indirectly sanctioned slavery. They rang the changes on the slogan "Liberty!" while holding millions in slavery.

The pre-Civil War debates over slavery are remarkable examples of constitutional hairsplitting. Did Congress have the right to outlaw slavery in the territories (where few slaves actually resided)? Did the people of a territory have a right to outlaw slavery *before* they wrote a state constitution or only *as* they wrote it? Congress and the people rarely debated about the evil where it existed (the Constitution protected it there) but about its constitutional right to go where it did not yet exist. Though the Second Great Awakening helped some Americans to confront the sins associated with slavery, many American political leaders were so chained to constitutional reasoning as to be unable to do so.

This blindness continues today in the form of a hypocritical interpretion of the Civil War. According to the popular interpretation, it was not a war caused by our national sin, but a noble conflict between Americans with honestly differing views of the Constitution—a conflict so noble that it somehow united Americans, North and South, even as they were killing each other. A tragedy is interpreted as an ennobling experience! As if there couldn't possibly be any other way to free slaves and unite the nation except by killing 600,000 fellow citizens—so we went ahead manfully and did what had to be done. Yet other nations freed their slaves with little if any bloodshed.

Contrast this view with Abraham Lincoln's Second Inaugural Address. Much of its eloquence comes from his confession that the Civil War was caused by the national sins associated with slavery. After quoting Jesus' saying (Matthew 18:7) about offences coming but woe to the man by whom they come, Lincoln applied it to the Civil War:

> If we shall suppose that American Slavery is one of those offences which, in the providence of God, must needs come, but which, having continued through His appointed time, He now wills to remove, and that He gives to both North and South, this terrible war, as the woe due to those by whom the offence came, shall we discern therein any departure from those divine attributes which the believers in a Living God always ascribe to Him?

Though he was as much given to constitutionalism as other political leaders, Lincoln had the ability to craft words that would pierce through the constitutional hairsplitting to the underlying moral issue.

After the war, constitutionalism limited Northerners' options as they debated how to secure the freedmen's future. They concluded that it was unconstitutional and illegal to confiscate private property in order to give each freed black family 40 acres and a mule, the means to self-sufficiency. The constitutional, democratic solution was simply to guarantee blacks the right to vote. To be given only the ballot (!) in a hostile society of Southern whites, and to be denied land, tools, jobs—everything needed to maintain independence and make the ballot meaningful! That recalls Jesus' ironic question: "Which of you, if his son asks for bread, will give him a stone?" (Matthew 7:9)

At least Northerners were well-intentioned in their desire to aid freed slaves after the Civil War. Their constitutionalism merely limited their ability to carry out their good intentions. Others in our history have hypocritically used constitutionalism as a cover to conceal immoral intentions.

> "You are like whitewashed tombs, which look beautiful on the outside but on the inside are full of dead men's bones and everything unclean." (Matthew 23:27b)

In the 1950s and 1960s, many Southerners again raised the cry of "states rights" and "strict construction" of the Constitution—and claimed their defense of segregation was a legal and constitutional one—while racial prejudice was clearly their main motive, while laws were being broken by their own police, and while constitutional guarantees of black suffrage were flagrantly violated at each election. It was the nonviolent civil rights marchers who revealed the hatred that motivated their opponents—in sharp contrast to the noble talk of constitutionalism. Bypassing the constitutional rhetoric, they used Martin Luther King's philosophy of non-violent direct action, which had its roots in Christ's teachings (as well as in Ghandi's and Thoreau's writings). The segregationists mouthed whitewashed slogans of constitutional rights while they denied rights to others, threatened or killed those who tried to claim their civil rights, and buried civil rights workers' bones in unmarked graves.

Thus, during the Civil War, during Reconstruction, and during the Civil Rights Movement of the 1950s and 1960s, constitutionalism became a transmitted tradition through which Americans ignored God's commands. We refused to confront the evils of slavery, failed to provide for the real physical needs of the freedmen, and did not repent of hatred and prejudice. Asking the question, "Is it constitutional?" became our way of avoiding the question, "Is it morally right?"

Similarly, since the 1973 Roe v. Wade decision, we have used constitutionalism as our tradition by which we set aside God's command about not taking innocent life. We mouth slogans about women's rights and the right to privacy. On the outside, this sloganeering appears "beautiful," but on the inside it is "full of dead men's bones" for it has been used to justify the killing of millions of unborn children. Those who try to point out the immorality of abortion are accused of fanaticism and extremism. The anti-abortion "extremists" have somehow failed to see that the issue is now one of jurisprudence, to be argued in terms of constitutional rights, and not one of morality. They have failed to set aside God's commands in favor of our American traditions. They thereby place themselves virtually outside the boundaries of public debate, at least as it is conducted at the universities or in the media.

Other examples of our constitutional hypocrisy could be named, such as interpreting nude dancing as a form of free speech, and interpreting the constitutional right to bear arms for militia or self-defense purposes as the right to own machine guns. It is clear, however, that we use our constitutional traditions and even make up new interpretations of the constitution to enable us to evade God's commands.

THE FALSE ARMAGEDDON: REPUBLICANS VS. DEMOCRATS

A third consequence of the false gospel of Americanism is that we reinterpret the struggle between good and evil as described in the Christian gospel to mean the struggle between Republicans and Democrats, between conservatives and liberals. If the nation has a near-messianic mission, then the question of which group will control the nation takes on enormous significance.

The Founders meeting in Philadelphia in the summer of 1787 did not plan for political parties, and they certainly did not write them into our Constitution. In his Farewell Address, George Washington warned Americans "against the baneful effects of the Spirit of Party." Despite initial anti-party feelings, in the 1790s Americans felt so deeply about their new experiment in republicanism that they divided sharply over how to conduct it. The two-party system was born. Ever since, this system has subtly encouraged Americans to view public affairs in terms of false dichotomies.

Currently, the two parties are divided over how to apply the traditional American belief in personal liberty—the right to be free from government restraint or regulation. Republicans apply it primarily in the economic sphere: entrepreneurs should be free to innovate and to operate from profit-seeking motives without fear of crippling government regulation or high taxation. Democrats apply freedom more to social, cultural and intellectual issues: artists and writers should be free from censorship or restraint; women should have reproductive freedom and the right to an abortion; no government-sanctioned morality should limit Americans' freedom to choose their own lifestyles.

Each party believes that somehow "the marketplace" will work. The economic marketplace will take individuals' greed and produce a widely-distributed prosperity. The marketplace of ideas will somehow produce truth out of the clash of mistaken sinners' opinions. "Let the market work," is what they both cry, but the market will not work to accomplish either goal.

Each party correctly accuses the other of being indifferent to the harmful consequences that the marketplace has on individuals. Republicans seem largely indifferent to poverty, unemployment and a grossly unequal distribution of income and wealth. Democrats appear indifferent to the moral chaos and the suffering resulting from irresponsible uses of social and cultural freedom: a high divorce rate, the widespread use of abortion as a form of birth control, the decline of the American family, the destructive effects of drug abuse and pornography.

This false dichotomy serves to divide Americans, including evangelical Christians, into two camps: those more concerned with social and economic justice, and those more concerned with personal morality and the "social issues." This is a false dichotomy, because the God Who reveals Himself in the Christian Gospel is concerned about *both* socioeconomic justice and personal morality, and He condemns that indifference to the fate of individuals which is part of *both* the Republican and Democratic philosophies. He is not indifferent. He does not value the marketplace above the fate of individuals.

By so elevating liberty and the marketplace above everything else, we hypocritically apply our traditions without regard to their effects on the lives of individuals. The constitutional or legal principle becomes, for us, more important than the individual. As Jesus said to the Pharisees, "You have a fine way of setting aside the commands of God in order to observe your own traditions!" (Mark 7:9) The liberal preaches social justice and deplores poverty while he encourages or allows the immoralities (e.g. drug and alcohol abuse, and sexual promiscuity) that often lead people into poverty. The conservative urges vigorous attacks on drugs and pornography while ignoring the ways in which poverty and unemployment often leave desperate people less able to resist temptations towards immorality.

It is sometimes said that Republicans and Democrats differ over the allocation of scarce resources. That can certainly be true when it comes to economic issues. More deeply, however, they differ over the allocation of a scarce morality. Republicans seek to allocate morality to the "social issues" while Democrats seek to allocate it to economic issues. We don't want to obey all of God's commands—the cultural and the economic, the personal and the social—so each of us chooses those few which we wish to obey. We then band together with like-minded sinners to insure that only those few become public policy. Our constitutionalism only makes it easier for us to artificially divide morality.

Nothing reveals the hollowness and the danger of this party fight more than the argument between Democrats and Republicans over our federal budget, that allocation of scarce resources and abundant needs. Democrats point to the ample social needs that must be met and occasionally invent new ones; Republicans point to the scarce tax revenues and enact tax cuts to make them even scarcer. With one party controlling the White House, and the other controlling Congress, they refuse to compromise and instead blame the other party for the nation's serious and growing federal budget deficit.

This deadlock insulates both parties from accountability because citizens can't figure out who is really to blame. It insulates us citizens from having to face fiscal realities—either through large tax increases or through deep spending cuts, or both. The Democratic Congress protects us from the consequences (deep spending cuts) of a low-tax policy while the Republican White House protects us from the consequences (high taxes) of a high-spending policy. This is a picture of a "checks-and-balances" system gone mad. Both White House and Congress resemble ships passing in the night more than separate branches of government checking each other for the common good.

The crowning irony is that what is terrible government turns out to be good politics for both parties. The Republicans can work one side of the street and appeal to overburdened taxpayers while the Democrats work the other side of the street and appeal to interest groups who feel that not enough federal spending is being allocated to the social need they are concerned about. Politicians from both parties can win re-election repeatedly. Winning control of both branches of government would expose them to the dangers of policy failure and accountability.

Political scientists and other experts, meanwhile, are hard put to condemn this fiscal irresponsibility, because that would mean defining the public good to mean, for example, a balanced or nearly-balanced budget. But that would contradict relativism. They accept, therefore, the idea that the public good is whatever the political parties define it as—provided they can obtain the voters' consent at the polls. So how can they then assign a higher value to any one definition of the public good?

We cannot shake this political relativism, even as the national debt climbs past $4 trillion and our attempts to tackle national problems are thereby stymied. Voter turnout is plummeting as a result of growing voter apathy and cynicism; only 50.2% of the eligible voters bothered to vote in the 1988 presidential election. We are praising ourselves for the triumph of democracy over dictatorship in Eastern Europe just as we are exhibiting less faith than ever in our own democracy's ability to solve that most basic governmental task—balancing the national budget.

THE FALSE THEOLOGY OF TODAY: DEMOCRATIC PLURALISM

The irony is that while we no longer trust democracy to do the basic governmental tasks such as balancing a budget, we have increasingly elevated Democracy into a near religion and entrusted it with the much more difficult and complex cultural tasks of providing personal fulfillment for individuals and insuring that minorities, the disabled, the poor, women and children are treated with respect and compassion. These tasks were previously left to Christianity and the church. Now, they are the tasks of a democratic philosophy of pluralism.

As a philosophy, pluralism is "spilled politics," a set of ideas originally found useful in politics and government and then applied indiscriminately to religion, sexuality, family relationships, education, and so forth. The two rallying cries of early 19th century political democracy—"freedom" and "equality"—have become demands of late 20th century cultural democracy; however, the meaning of the terms has significantly changed.

For the purposes of conducting elections, a democracy takes its very diverse group of citizens and considers them each abstractly as one political unit, one voter. Each one's vote counts the same despite the diversities, as it should. Similarly, when considered as a taxpayer, a defendant, a soldier, a recipient of money—or in any other relationship to the government—each is to be treated equally without any preference or prejudice based on his or her personal characteristics. Each is considered as an abstraction, a citizen without personal characteristics as it were.

Each political unit—each citizen—has rights equal to those of every other unit, which is as it should be. Yet, when considering that individual's roles as sexual partner, parent or child, student or teacher, such abstractions, such a filtering out of personal, sexual and intellectual characteristics may not be helpful at all, but may distort our thinking about such non-political roles.

Perhaps the best example is the feminist movement and its approach to women's reproductive role and "reproductive rights." Mimicking politics and its concept of equal political rights for all citizens, feminists have attempted to guarantee equal "reproductive rights" for both women and men, despite the obvious fact that nature assigns completely opposite reproductive roles to the two sexes. The (possible) physical consequences of sexual intercourse fall entirely upon the female in the form of a pregnancy, whether wanted or unwanted.

In order to give the female citizen an abstract "reproductive right" and a position of abstract equality with the male citizen, feminists grant to her the very unnatural "right" to destroy her own child. Yet the damaging physical, emotional and spiritual consequences of exercizing that "right" fall upon the female much more than upon the male who fathered the child.

The recent Supreme Court decision in Planned Parenthood v. Casey demonstrates the distorted, one-dimensional reasoning that results from the attempt to make all citizens and all rights abstractly equal. Ignoring the woman's vertical relationship with her Creator and her horizontal relationships with the people in her life, Justices O'Connor, Kennedy and Souter, in their majority opinion, focus solely on the woman-citizen's relationship with the state. They seem to equate woman's role in childbearing with any volunteer job, which "ennobles her in the eyes of others," but whose ennobling results "cannot alone be grounds for the state to insist she make the sacrifice." The woman need not inform her husband or, unless she is a minor, anyone else in her life. She need only give the state 24 hours notice. To make the woman abstractly equal to males, the state gives her this "right"—well-knowing that she will be hurt most by exercizing it. Reacting to this decision, one pro-choice congresswoman equated the right to abort with the right to vote! If we don't restrict one, we shouldn't restrict the other! Voting may end some politician's career; abortion surely ends a life-in-the-making. To equate the two reveals how an obsession with abstract equality distorts moral perceptions.

These abstract concepts of democracy are totally inadequate to protect the woman from sexual exploitation and its consequences. Traditionally, Christianity taught males that it was wrong to exploit women, and that they would face painful spiritual consequences if they did so. Now, this "spilled politics" of equality (where there is a complete difference in roles) has removed these restraints while itself failing to protect women.

A democracy that cannot restrain economic greed will somehow be able to restrain a much stronger sexual greed!

Similarly, political pluralism has been "spilled" onto the cultural sphere and converted into a philosophy of life. (I am not arguing that politics and culture should be in two different compartments whose contents should never be allowed to mix.) A limited degree of pluralism is helpful when debating and deciding the ordinary governmental issues in a democracy. No one political opinion should be privileged, but all opinions should be given a hearing. There is no one correct opinion on which street should be paved first or which agency's budget should be trimmed first, or which tax should be raised and which lowered.

There are limits to how far pluralism can be extended. First, when government makes rulings that go beyond its ordinary tasks to deal with questions of morality, of life and death, then it begins to be less helpful to grant all opinions an absolutely equal role in the debate. A skinhead may not have as good (as "equal") an opinion on street crime as a Good Samaritan.

Secondly, we Americans have "spilled" our politics by projecting our idea of democracy onto the cosmos: if every citizen has an equally valid opinion on where the sewer lines should be laid, then each one's opinion on the origins of the universe or the meaning of life is also equally valid. Just because our township is run on democratic lines does not mean the universe is too. Yet, many Americans see our democratic, pluralistic philosophy as ruling out the traditional Christian claim to exclusive truth, the claim that "there is one God, and one mediator between God and men, the man Christ Jesus" (1 Timothy 2:5). Even if a democratic philosophy succeeds in governing one country (and ours isn't succeeding that well), it cannot possibly disprove the truth that the Sovereign Lord governs the universe.

Yet, with our philosophy of pluralism, we have elevated democracy into a theology, or, rather, an anthropology, for it elevates man into the place of God. *Vox populi, vox dei.* The voice of the people is the voice of God. In our provincialism, we imagine that the principle which governs our nation must govern the universe also.

The final element in this "spilled politics" is the way in which the traditional democratic politician's flattery towards the voters (the best, the most generous, the kindest, the hardest-working people, etc.) becomes pluralism's more general flattery towards the individual (everyman his own philosopher), the corporations' flattery towards the consumer, and even the minister's flattery towards the congregation. It becomes increasingly difficult to tell the plain truth to people, because they are so unused to hearing it.

Jeremiah was told to speak out against the false prophets of prosperity:

> Do not listen to what the prophets are prophesying to you; they fill you with false hopes . . . . They keep saying to those who despise Me, "The Lord says: You will have peace." And to all who follow the stubbornness of their hearts they say, "No harm will come to you." (Jeremiah 23:16–17)

In another passage, the Lord Himself criticizes them:

> A horrible and shocking thing has happened in the land;
> The prophets prophesy lies, the priests rule by their own authority
> and My people love it this way.
> But what will you do in the end?
> (Jeremiah 5:30–31)

Of course, the citizens in a democracy "love it this way," but the last question is the key point—"what will you do in the end?" In the end, the flattery will turn out false and useless.

THE FALSE TWINS: AMERICANISM AND CHRISTIANITY

> Did the word of God originate with you? Or are you the only people it has reached? (1 Corinthians 14:36)

I grew up as an identical twin, who was often mistaken for someone else. In current public debate, evangelical Christianity and Americanism are often regarded as virtually identical twins, difficult to tell apart because they look alike and difficult to separate because they grew up together and are attached to each other.

There is a marked tendency in American society to regard evangelical Christianity as a creation of American culture, a faith that characterized certain periods in the American past and certain regions of America, but that now is an irrelevant, out-dated relic. Some evangelical Christians see their faith as deeply embedded in American history and culture, to the point where Americanism and Christianity can hardly be separated.

Both tendencies confuse Americanism with Christianity. Both are barriers to Americans truly understanding and accepting the Good News of Jesus Christ. Both result from the superficial similarities between the gospel of Americanism and the Christian gospel: the new birth, the chosen people, the sacred texts, the divine mission. We have already traced the ways in which these similarities developed, and the degree to which they are false similarities. Only a few additional observations are needed.

First, let us accept as self-evident the proposition that belief in the Deity and the Messianic claims of Jesus of Nazareth, Who lived in first-century Palestine, so far predates the formation of the United States of America as to make it quite anachronistic to suppose that His message is closely linked to Americanism. The Christian church existed for over 1500 years before the Pilgrims landed at Plymouth.

Evangelical Christianity has flourished in America for almost 400 years now. In that time, certain of its characteristics have embedded themselves so deeply in American society as to take on the appearance of American traits, and certain characteristics of American society have come to so characterize American

Christians as to seem uniquely Christian instead of only uniquely American.

Actually, the problem is more complex than that. Evangelicalism is not simply identified with America as a whole. Evangelical Christianity has been so dominant at certain periods and in certain regions that it is identified in the secular mind with those periods of American history and those regions within America, and they with it.

Puritan New England was a strongly Christian society. Evangelical Christianity has, therefore, the reputation of being Puritanical—another anachronism. Having its origins in Judaism and not Puritanism, evangelical Christianity's emphasis on high standards of personal morality derives from the same emphasis in ancient Judaism. The truth that God is a holy God Who demands purity and morality is an ancient truth, not one invented in 17th century New England. Superficial analyses of the supposed puritanical nature of the American people ignore the fact that devout people in all ages and places have stressed purity and morality.

Take two other examples. During the Second Great Awakening in the early 19th century, evangelical Christianity succeeded in winning many converts on the frontier. The camp meeting and the circuit-riding Methodist preacher were fixtures of frontier America in the 1820s and 1830s. Both institutions lacked intellectual refinement, and encouraged anti-intellectual attitudes. Evangelical Christianity became identified in many minds with everything that was anti-intellectual. Yet evangelicals founded numerous colleges, encouraged intellectual activity, and numbered many intellectuals among their followers.

Similarly, many people identify fundamentalist Christianity with anti-urban, backwoods people living in the so-called "Bible

Belt" in the 1920s. Pre-millenialism, which was the predecessor to fundamentalism, was begun by highly-educated, literate, urban clergy and laity in the 19th century—and many were Englishmen, not Americans. Neither evangelicalism nor fundamentalism are inherently anti-intellectual or anti-urban.

Writing about the 1920s, one historian has referred to Christian ideas of personal morality as "local values" in contrast to the "modern values" of sexual freedom, equality for women, consumerism and urban lifestyles.[7] Actually, beliefs in premarital chastity and abstention from mind-altering drugs, for example, are so prevalent across the globe—in Papua New Guinea, the Farøe Islands, southwestern Norway, the rural South—that they are not "local" at all, but simply a set of cosmopolitan, global values that happen to be different than the cosmopolitan values that the historian and his fellow "moderns" might prefer. But they are no less cosmopolitan because the historian finds them undesirable. They are found wherever Christianity has achieved significant influence on a society.

The Gospel transcends any particular time or place. It should not be surprising that people attempt to enlist the Gospel to defend their traditional or local attitudes and to guarantee the status quo, but that does not make the Gospel itself "traditional" or "local." The "Old Time Religion" has been so used in the South to defend traditions of racial prejudice and white supremacy. That does not make the Gospel racist. Gospel preaching resulted in numerous conversions among Southern slaves despite opposition from white slaveholders. That is impressive testimony to the power of the Holy Spirit to overflow the river banks of human prejudice and to flood the land when and where He chooses. People have tried to use the Gospel to defend the status quo, but the transforming power of the Gospel has transcended their efforts.

What must Christians then do to dispel the illusion our culture is continually trying to create—the illusion that Americanism and Christianity are inextricably linked?

We must first warn individuals that being an American, even a patriotic one, does not save anyone from the various hazards and corrupting vices of modern life. Americanism is powerless to save.

We must warn our society against "spilling" politics into every corner of American life. We must continually warn that while democracy is indeed useful in making decisions about budgets and priorities in city hall and in the Congress, it cannot be extrapolated into an all-compassing philosophy that applies to the most intimate details of family life as well as to the most infinite reaches of the cosmos. We must warn Americans that though the "people love it this way . . . what will you do in the end?"

We must warn ourselves not to attempt a theocracy, a government of the saints. Democracy is not a vehicle to put the Church in power. Sinners will never vote to put the saints in power in order to outlaw sin. Even if they did, we shouldn't accept it. Politics and government are based on coercive power, and the Church must never be tempted to use coercive power to compel religious belief or behavior. Though the universe is not run on the principle of pluralism, it can be a temporarily useful principle to run a country on, for it provides freedom of religious choice for the individual. Lesslie Newbigin reminds us,

> It is the will of the Father to provide a space and time wherein men and women can give their allegiance to the kingdom in the only way it can be given—namely, in freedom. To use the God-given authority of the state to deny that freedom is thus to violate the

space God himself has provided and put into the care of earthly governors.[8]

Though we must remind men and women that their freedom is not a permanent law of the universe akin to the law of gravity, we must not take it from them.

We must remind ourselves that, in the final sense, this is not our country. We are resident aliens just as the faithful have been through all generations:

> And they admitted that they were aliens and strangers on earth. People who say such things show that they are looking for a country of their own. If they had been thinking of the country they had left, they would have had opportunity to return. Instead, they were longing for a better country—a heavenly one. Therefore God is not ashamed to be called their God, for he has prepared a city for them. (Hebrews 11:13b–16)

We must remind ourselves that any attempts to construct a coalition to save the United States will inevitably involve the risk of accommodation with "the public faith's deistic unitarianism which ignores the scandal of the cross." It is the cross that most clearly shows that our Lord was and is politically rejected. We must share in His political rejection until He returns:

> And so Jesus also suffered outside the city gate to make the people holy through his own blood. Let us, then, go to him outside the camp, bearing the disgrace he bore. For here we do not have an enduring city. (Hebrews 13:12–14)

Finally, we must remember His ultimate sovereignty. F.F. Bruce reports that when British monarchs are crowned, they are given "a golden orb surmounted by a cross," and these words are solemnly spoken to them: "When you see the orb set under the cross, remember that the whole world is subject to the power and empire of Christ our Redeemer." In this country where the people are the sovereigns, we Christians need to constantly remind them of that same fact.

13

"LUCKY IS THE LITTLE HISTORIAN"

"LYKKELIG ER DEN LILLE SKJALD"(GRUNDTVIG)

Lucky is the little historian,
Reading Classic Comics on Lincoln, Boone.
A general riding his bike up the road,
He orders reinforcements to come soon.
Retired, he argues the Civil War
While weeding carrots with his twin brother.
The cods of dirt they threw at each other
Exploded in little brown puffs of dust.
The rows of peas and corn a battlefield—
Siloh, Pea Ridge, or Antietam's cornfield.
He never thought he'd live to write a book.
Lucky is the little historian.

In the living room, an English preacher,
Who, he imagined, was Winston Churchill,
Told stories of desert war and Rommel,

Capture at Torbruk, German prison camps.
Desert winds cast blinding sand in his eyes,
A dim light came from the living room lamps
As he listened late into the night.
Lucky is the little historian,
Who escaped the war others had to fight,
Wrote a book on a man he never knew,
Imagining the past like he used to do,
To extend his life back before his birth.

Lucky is the little historian,
Thus become older the his oldest brother,
Recalling what mother's too young to know,
Seeing places his aunt's too young to go,
Telling his father things that had happened
Before either of them was even born.
Lucky is the little historian,
Who sees his work as a Classic Comic
Compared to the Father's magnum opus
(History as seen by the Ancient of Days),
The little historian's personal praise
Exalts the history of the Only Son.

14

YOUR PAST IS OUR PRESENT

Tuesday and Wednesday, 20 and 21 August 1991, were strange days to be researching history in New Ulm, Minnesota. Inside the Brown County Historical Society building, the Hanska-Linden Cooperative Store was increasing its trade and its sales force throughout the 1890s and early 1900s. Annual meetings were opened, lunches served, directors elected, and adjournment resolutions carried. Outside, my car radio brought the latest news from Moscow. Boris Yeltsin was increasing his popular force outside the Russian Parliament building, and Russian politicians were coming down with "coup flu."

At 10 PM Tuesday night, I left my tent at Flandrau State Park to listen to the CBS news reports on my car radio. It was early Wednesday morning in Moscow and the tanks seemed about to move on the crowds gathered behind the barricades. Around noon on Wednesday, as I drove to the Ulmer Cafe for lunch, the car radio carried the remarkable news that the coup leaders had fled Moscow and the drama was over. Sipping some soup at the Ulmer, I was moved to read in the "counter copy" newspaper that when the tanks seemed poised to strike, the crowds prayed and placed pictures of Christ on the barricades.

Rarely, in my experience, has the history happening in the present so completely overshadowed the history recorded in the past.

People sometimes equate the study of history with nostalgia—as if those who study the past romanticize it and try to escape the present with its confusion and anxiety. It's often the other way around. It's the city dweller who visits the woods once a year who is most likely to romanticize the forest, not the trapper or logger who works there year round. So also, it's often not the historian, who works in the past year round and in his or her research frequently encounters stories of past suicides and murders and scandals, who tends to romanticize the past. It's the banker, the salesman, or the machinist who stops at a museum while vacationing and longingly looks at the relics of the simple rural life led by his grandparents.

It's not that summers spent traveling around Minnesota and researching rural cooperatives haven't turned up pleasant and nostalgic experiences: evening walks around Fountain Lake in Albert Lea and past the Danish immmigrant statue in the park, a small 1940s resort on Lake Lida with three booths and great burgers, a 1930s-style coffee shop in Fergus Falls where any concern about a constant diet of coffee and rolls seems out of place, a 19th-century flour mill at Phelps with the cobwebbed machinery still in place.

NOSTALGIA AT THE WESTERN STEAM THRESHERS REUNION

Perhaps the greatest temptation to nostalgia came at the Western Steam Threshers Reunion (WMSTR) at Rollag. The WMSTR is sort of a State Fair designed by rural people for rural people: no paid professional staffers, no commercialization, 1600 volunteers, no parking fees, no celebrities, free admission for kids under 12. They expected 70,000 people that year. It looked like they would get that number and more.

Puffing clouds of black smoke out of its "old stogie" of a smokestack, an old steam locomotive pulls a passenger train around a railroad track that circles a small lake and the rest of the 240 acre WMSTR site, and passes through "Buttzville" (the rest rooms), Lutefisk Junction, and Pleasant Valley. At the horsepowered farm beyond the Hitterdal depot, a team of four horses pulls a reaper that rhythmically beats down the golden wheat stalks.

At 10 AM, over 400 antique tractors and machines—both gas and steam-powered—parade up the hill and past the reviewing "stand" (where the announcer stands in the second-floor window of the white headquarters building). There is no Grand Marshal. Each driver of each tractor is equal to every other driver—and many have their children or their wife along for the ride—and many women drive too. Toward the end of the parade come the great behemoths, the steam threshing tractors, with wheels six to eight feet high and the wooden roof as high as the roof of your house. Looking like Rube Goldberg contraptions, some with what looks like your home furnace in front, and all with belts, wheels, chains, and whistles going at once—they belch black smoke and crawl up the hill at 6 mph. Using 20 foot belts, these gargantuan tractors power the threshing machines and the saw mill during the threshing (pronounced "thrashing") and sawmilling demonstrations that follow the parade.

The WMSTR motto for this year: "Your Past is Our Present."

That is the historian's motto, too. The histories of the Sverdrup and Manchester Mutual Insurance Companies, and of the Hanska-Linden Cooperative Store, were my summer tasks. And the WMSTR helped me to envision the past—to see what Olaf Aune, Iver A. Rodsater, and Ole Narveson were doing when they weren't busy attending board meetings. But that doesn't mean that I long to be doing the same things.

First, they weren't only driving tractors and threshing grain. Nostalgia takes the unpleasantness out of the past and retains only good memories. The WMSTR is sort of a self-constructed paradise for that generation of males who were most comfortable talking about machines. The things they liked to talk about are basically the only things that exist in the WMSTR's recreated world. What has been left out are the unpleasant subjects: lonely wives waiting for threshermen to return, sick children, grown-up sons eager to strike out for Minneapolis, a mountain of debts.

Frenquently, as the historian searches through century-old newspapers, the unpleasant subjects show up. An editor's wife runs off with a local minister. They head for England, but are headed off in New York, where her relatives discover them traveling under assumed names and haul the minister back to Waseca on charges of absconding with church funds. One of the families is broken by the subsequent divorce.

Second, Olaf Aune and Iver Rodsater and Ole Narveson probably took steam threshing and cooperative general stores just about as far as those ideas could go. The designers of Advance-Rumely steam threshing tractors probably made all the design improvements that could be made in those behemoths. The gasoline engine made a different approach necessary. There is no sense in worshipping technology just at a certain stage in its development, no sense in freezing it at a supposedly simple and pure stage and then romanticizing that machine—to look longingly back at it.

Third, those onlookers admiring the Advance-Rumely tractors are probably no less eager than their neighbors to buy the latest International Harvester combine. Nostalgia is not at all opposed to the idea of progress, to the idea that modern is better. As Christopher Lasch notes in his recent book *The True and Only Heaven*, nostalgia does not "assert the superiority of bygone days," but instead, in "exaggerating the naive simplicity of earlier times, it implicitly celebrates the worldly wisdom of later generations." The historian seeks to understand the continuing influence of the past on the present, not to freeze the past at a certain stage of development and then admire it. Nostalgia, writes Lasch,

> evokes the past only to bury it alive. It shares with the belief in progress, to which it is only superficially opposed, an eagerness to proclaim the death of the past and to deny history's hold over the present. Those who mourn the death of the past and those who acclaim it both take for granted that our age has outgrown its childhood.

Like the historian and unlike the nostalgic person, the Christian ought to acknowledge the past's continuing impact on the present and to deny that "our age" can outgrow God's revelation which He spoke, after all, in the past.

Fourth, like waves washing away my sons' sand castles by Sakatah Lake each day, so time tends to erase the dreams, ideas, and accomplishments of each generation in turn. It does not erase their influence over the future, but that future turns out to be very different that what they envisioned.

When writing a biography of Hjalmar Petersen during the early 1980s, I was strongly struck by the way in which the 1930s hopes of the Farmer-Laborites had been washed away by later events. In 1985, the Cooperative Commonwealth, pacifism, disarmament, and an end to capitalism could hardly have seemed farther from realization. As a biographer, I stood on the pinnacle of hindsight and philosophized about the failed hopes of the Farmer-Laborites, which appeared as mere wisps in the distance behind me. Little did I realize then that my own ideas, so firmly rooted in my Cold War upbringing, were so soon to be outdated themselves. After the Russian revolution of August 1991 and the breakup of the Soviet Union, Cold War ideas were washed away. The Cuban Missile Crisis of 1962 seemed like ages ago. While sipping some sauerkraut soup at the Ulmer Cafe and reading about Russians manning barricades against Red Army tanks, I felt that even 1985 seemed a distant memory.

It is not hard to predict that future events will also wash away the euphoric hopes aroused by the recent end to the Cold War, and the democratization of Eastern Europe and the Soviet Union. These hopes will not be realized in the end. There was war before communism and there will be war after it is gone.

The historian is not nostalgic about the past, but realistic about the present. Present-minded wheelers and dealers act as if their sand castles will be the marvel of future generations. The historian realizes that time and change will very likely erase even their footprints.

DETERMINISM AND THE FUTURE OF RURAL MINNESOTA

This realization, however, leaves the historian susceptible to indifference or cynicism or to a deterministic fatalism. The "objective" historian is not supposed to care about the fate of the older, rural Minnesota, for example.

Mingling with the crowds who were eager to see the steam-threshing exhibition and who thronged onto the WMSTR train then driving through the countryside, I was struck by the contrast between a bustling, populated rural Minnesota of 1890, at the height of the Farmers' Alliance movement, and the depopulated countryside of 1990. It is a cliche, but farm country has increasingly become a food factory, in which machines are much more numerous than people. Driving between Lakefield and Worthington, I was shocked to see a dozen or so people with hoes out in a field of corn. I almost stopped the car to ask what they thought they were doing there.

Our highly-mechanized, large-scale agriculture is the main cause. We could just shrug our shoulders and say it's inevitable. Progress determines technology and its scale. Free market economics gives us whole lists of reasons why such changes are inevitable and encourages us to shrug our shoulders at our neighbors' economic misfortunes. "Get big or get out" has been the slogan of American agriculture. Still, the words of Isaiah are disturbing: "Woe to those who add house to house and join field to field until everywhere belongs to them and they are the sole inhabitants of the land" (Isaiah 5:8).

Making moral judgments between past ways and present ways is not necessarily nostalgic. Honesty forces us to conclude that past ways are sometimes morally preferable to current ones.

In a moral sense, the good thing about that "wonderful picnicking, speech-making Alliance summer of 1890" was that people believed their neighbors' economic misfortunes were their concern too. To meet the agricultural crisis, the low commodity prices and the drought, farmers and their wives banded together in the Farmers' Alliance, and in the many new cooperative organizations. They did not accept the inevitability of their neighbors' eventual failure, but together tried to find a way out. Sure, they made some mistakes. Perhaps they put too much faith in government's ability to solve their problems. But they did not accept determinism, that morally-deadening idea that destroys neighborliness—the idea that their neighbor must be at fault for his economic misfortunes and should not be given a hand.

It is hard not to be impressed by the efforts of farmers meeting in their local township hall or district school house, forming Alliances and cooperatives, trusting each other to the extent of co-signing bank notes, and discussing their common problems at weekly Saturday night meetings. By contrast, our free market economy often does not wear such a neighborly human face, except in carefully-contrived TV commercials in which lovable babies are cynically set to work polishing the image of large multinational corporations. It is not nostalgia to find neighborliness morally superior to self-centered consumerism.

When and where are we going to draw the line and say that rural depopulation has gone too far? The rural writer Wendell Berry argues that agriculture cannot be treated as just another industry:

> The "free market"—the unbridled play of economic forces—is bad for agriculture because it is unable to assign a value to things that are necessary to agriculture. It gives a value to agricultural products, but it cannot give a value to the sources of those products in the topsoil, the ecosystem, the farm, the farm family, or the farm community.[1]

It also cannot assign a value to spiritual concerns, to our worship of God, to prayer. It is not nostalgia to point out that this failure to value family, community, and church characterizes the present more than the past.

> The picture is not all gloomy. There are many farm communities that have succeeded. The Danish-American community of Clarks

Grove near Albert Lea appears to be doing well. I attended a concert given by a men's quartet at their Baptist church, a very impressive building for a community of 600. They just celebrated the 100th anniversary of the town and a local historian has written a good town history for the centennial. Clarks Grove is famous for its community spirit. By sticking together, they even forced the railroad to move its depot into town, because they refused to go to the speculator's town site where the railroad originally placed the depot. Strong communities can still be built on faith, family and neighborliness.

Nostalgia or even neighborliness, however, is no long-range answer to the despair that comes from witnessing continual moral decline and the destruction of traditional values. We can only endure in the long run if we put our hope in One whose plans are not washed away by events. While sitting by Fountain Lake in Albert Lea, I found this passage in the Psalms: "The Lord foils the plans of the nations . . . . But the plans of the Lord stand firm forever, the purposes of His heart through all generations" (Psalm 33:10–11). The Lord foils the post-communism New World Order, but His plans stand firm.

HANSKA, KRISTOFER JANSON AND HISTORY

On a blustery and bitter-cold January afternoon, I drove west from Mankato along the snow-covered back roads towards Hanska. Snow was falling and accumulating fast by the time I drove up the hill (Mt. Pisquah) on which stood Nora Unitarian Church. A blizzard was blowing in from the west.

Because of my wrong turn at Lake Crystal, I was fifteen or thirty minutes late. Hurrying down the driveway to the parsonage, I slipped on the icy slope and fell on my kiester—note cards and folders flying every which way—just as the Unitarian minister came out for a look.

She continued farther up the hill to the church, where she soon located the church minutes for me. I was researching the history of a cooperative store in Hanska, and thought the church minutes would prove useful. We walked over to an unheated log cabin, a summertime museum, to search for more minute books. Sticking the three-inch long key into a 19th-century immigrant's trunk, we pulled and pushed for a good twenty minutes. My fingers felt near the frostbite stage when the lid finally lifted.

What I wanted was not inside the trunk, but the minister kindly invited me inside the parsonage to warm up and to do my note-taking. She offered me the use of the desk in the pastor's study, with bookshelves stretching from floor to ceiling and with portraits of Unitarian ministers hanging on the walls. It felt strange to sit there with the heroes of Unitarianism looking solemnly down at me. They looked as surprised as I was.

Started in 1881–82, Nora Fri-kristne Menighed (Nora Unitarian Church) was the result of a bitter quarrel among the Norwegian-American farmers who belonged to the Lake Hanska Lutheran congregation. The issue was where to build their church. According to Norwegian custom, the church and the cemetery should be at the same site. However, a majority of the congregation now lived to the west of the cemetery. They voted to build a church one-half mile west of the cemetery.

That was too much. The congregation split over the issue. The dissenters contacted Kristofer Janson, a newly-ordained Unitarian minister newly-immigrated from Norway, and constructed a new church building (east of the cemetery). Though these Hanska farmers had no trouble abandoning a belief in hell and in the inspiration of the Bible, they balked at abandoning "their faith in the divinity of Christ." Janson smoothly reassured them that "if it was truth for them" then they could retain it, while he led them into affiliating with the Unitarians, who denied it. Ironically, the name Kristofer (or, Christopher) means "Christ-bearer."

Secure in his own new church, Janson announced that on Sunday, July 22, he would preach a sermon disproving the deity of Jesus Christ. On Saturday morning, July 21, the sky "grew darker, lightning flashed and a strong wind arose." As the Janson family and some carpenters sat in the Jansons' unfinished house, a tornado hit and sent "the walls and the roof . . . flying down the hill" and then the floor too—"sending the sixteen people on it through the air and then dropping them onto the wreckage." Thankfully, no one was seriously hurt, though some were bruised. In the following hailstorm, the Nora church itself was hit by lightning and then likewise sent "flying through the air."[2]

According to one Lutheran version of events, Kristofer Janson then picked himself up from the brush and said, "Our God is angry today."

That was exactly the Lutheran interpretation. A letter signed "A Lutheran" and titled "God Will Not Be Mocked At" ("Gud lader sig ikke spotte") appeared in the Norwegian-American newspaper *Nordvesten.* Janson had tried to "spit God straight in the face," said the writer, but the tornado threw "the church of the blasphemer from its foundation." Ironically, that same tornado caused the Lake Hanska Lutheran church to be "swung from its foundation a couple of rods at one end" and "its front is out of line with the road to this day."

Kristofer Janson quickly recovered his emotional balance and even his irreverent wit. When one Lutheran wrote to him and asked, "Pastor! Are you the Antichrist who is to come, or should we expect another," Janson wrote back, "It is best to wait for another." According to his biographer Nina Draxten, he later deserted his wife Drude (who was in love with another man), ran off with a woman who was a spiritualist medium, and returned to Norway in some disgrace.

They would have to wait for another. Janson was quite able to self-destruct without the benefit of a tornado. (Ironically, a tornado later severely damaged his Minneapolis church as well.)

Knowing the strange history of that hill, that congregation, and that Unitarian minister, I felt strange sitting at the desk in the pastor's study and reading the old church minutes. I recalled when I was in my twenties, rebelling against the seeming impossibility of my leading the Christian life, in love with a young woman who attended a Unitarian church, sitting in Unity Church in St. Paul, listening to those very rational sermons, and singing those abstract, de-spiritualized hymns. How could I tell my father that I had fallen in love with a young woman who attended a Unitarian church?

Yet, at least the Unitarians were not hypocritical. We have all attended churches that acknowledged the Trinity in their creed yet were just as impersonal and de-spiritualized as a Unitarian hymn. We have too often tamed and domesticated the awesome reality of the deity of Christ. At Christmas, we treat the Incarnation like a "warm fuzzy," like God's hug of the human family, instead of the rescuing Heimlich maneuver that it is.

It is possible to be Unitarian in practice, when we aren't in creed. It is possible to have our foundation only moved a few rods instead of being totally blown away by this reality. I can remember encountering the reality of the Son while singing the hymn "I've Found a Friend"—and while listening to a radio sermon while driving past Concordia College and the Prairie Home Cemetery in Moorhead—and it felt more like being emotionally lifted up and tossed through the air and set down somewhere totally other than where I had been before.

The early Christians were described as "These that have turned the world upside down." We are often more like the Hanska farmers, who regarded Christ's deity only as "truth for them," not truth for everyone—and then gave it up even for themselves.

The Nora Church survived Janson's move into spiritualism; so did the rivalry between it and Lake Hanska Lutheran. After the new village of Hanska was built in 1900, the Lutheran congregation decided to build a church in town so as to better compete with the Unitarians, who were located only one-half mile from the village. The Nora congregation then retaliated by building on a prominent Hanska street corner the Liberal Union Hall, from which they could wage their struggle for the hearts and minds of Hanska's citizens.

What really irritated the Norwegian-American Lutherans was that Janson regarded himself and his beliefs as the harbinger of the future. History was on his side. He eagerly embraced numerous causes—the move to outlaw capital punishment, Christian Socialism, and spiritualism—and believed them to be enlightened. He clearly regarded the Norwegian-American Lutheran clerics as relics of the past, destined to be superseded, along with their beliefs in the divinity of Jesus Christ, the everlasting punishment of the wicked, and the divine inspiration of the Scriptures.

It turned out to be Janson himself who was superseded.

As Christopher Lasch points out, both nostalgia and a belief in progress—or, a belief that *your* views will be the ones to progress—contain serious flaws in their approach to both the past and the future. Nostalgia, determinism, and a foolish faith in progress are all alike flawed.[3]

The Gospel holds out the unflawed alternatives. It offers respect for the decent values of the past and for the past's continuing influence on the present. It does not both praise and bury the past, as nostalgia does. It commands repentence where present conduct falls short of those values. Instead of a technological determinism operating regardless of fairness or love, it proclaims the kingdom values that are triumphing because they are fair and loving. Instead of encouraging passivity, it instructs us that we must act on behalf of those values—even though they are destined to triumph. Not foolishly optimistic, the Gospel offers us faith and hope: "Now faith is being sure of what we hope for and certain of what we do not see" (Hebrews 11:1). Finally, this hope is grounded in the sure knowledge that "the plans of the Lord stand firm forever, the purposes of his heart through all generations."

15

JEG FANDT EN VEN

Jeg fandt en Ven, o hvilken Ven!
Jeg aldrig fer Ham kendte;
Han ved sin store kærlighed
Mit hjeerte til sig vendte.
Han bandt mit hjerte fast med bånd,
Som intet sønderriver,
Nu er jeg Hans, og Han er min,
Og min Han evigt bliver.

Jeg fandt en Ven, o hvilken Ven!
Hans død mig skænked' livet,
Hans sejr er min, Hans live er mit,
Han har sig selv mig givet.
Jeg derfor nu til Ham igen
Det alt tilbage giver,
Så jeg med legem', ånd og sjæl
Er Hans og Hans forbliver.

Jeg fandt en Ven, o hvilken Ven
Så tro, så god og kærlig,
Med hjælp Han er mig altid nær,

An er min Frelser herlig;
Så vist jeg ved, at ingen magt
Ud af Hans hand mig river
I sorg og glæde, liv og død
Jeg Hans for evig bliver.

16

SINCE THEY HAVE REJECTED THE WORD OF THE LORD, WHAT KIND OF WISDOM DO THEY HAVE?

"The poststructuralists first attacked Saussure's understanding of the sign as the union of a word (the signifier) and the idea or object for which it stands (the signified). For Jacques Derrida, Roland Barthes, and others, this presumed unity is a fiction; signifiers are not bonded to signifieds; they merely point to other signifiers . . . we are left with an endless chain of signifiers in which meaning is always deferred and finally absent. There is no external point of reference, *no ultimate word . . . that will ground meaning, guaranteeing it once and for all.*"[1]

Don't be too discouraged if you don't understand this opening quotation. It is only a statement of the problem. You will understand the answer at the end, if not the problem.

In its June 1989 issue, the *American Historical Review* featured a series of five essays under the general title, "AHR Forum: The Old History and the New." These essays had originally been delivered as papers at a meeting of the American Historical Association. In addition, this issue of the *AHR* included another

"Forum" on the subject of intellectual history; this debate touched on some of the same issues as did "The Old History and the New." Combined, they provide an excellent view of the modern "crisis" in the historical profession and in modern scholarship generally.

I will not discuss this crisis except to summarize it. However, some comments by David Harlan positively invite a brief critique of this crisis in light of the Christian idea of the Logos. Harlan introduces religious ideas in a metaphorical sense, without realizing the literal application that could be made. The opportunity to apply these ideas literally is too tempting to pass up.

THE POLITICAL CRISIS IN THE HISTORICAL PROFESSION

The crisis of the historical profession in America is both a "political" one and a linguistic one. According to Gertrude Himmelfarb's contribution to the *AHR* Forum, the political crisis results from the desire of many groups (e.g., "blacks, women, Chicanos, American Indians, immigrants . . .") to rewrite American history in their own terms, in order to place themselves at the center of it.

Himmelfarb argues that the result is chaos: "In the democratic ethos of the new history, no subject, no theme, no question wants to take second place to any other." Group historians rework the past into whatever pattern is most politically useful to that group. They surround the word "fact" with sneering quotation marks. They come close to denying "the reality of the historical past," close to putting words in the mouths of historical actors. As a result, there is no widely agreed upon version of the past, only a series of minority versions.

We Minnesotans could call it "walking subcaucus" history. In our DFL (Democratic-Farmer-Labor) party conventions, the whole body of delegates doesn't nominate, discuss, vote on, and (thus) agree to a slate of delegates to the next highest convention. Instead, individuals break out into self-selected groups identified by a candidate's name (e.g., Jones for President) or by a position on the issues (e.g., Prolife). These separate groups or subcaucuses then nominate, discuss, and vote separately. Individuals "walk" from one subcaucus to the other until they find one that is "viable," one which has enough supporters to elect one delegate to the next convention. There is no one group of delegates whom the convention as a whole selects and agrees upon, merely separate groups separately selected. Critics charge that the convention becomes, not a deliberative body debating and finally acting, but a mere hall in which sub-groups meet, and the convention's minutes, mere documents in which sub-groups' decisions are recorded.

Similarly, in the historical profession, individual historians "walk" from one historians' sub-group to another until they find one with which they can identify. That sub-group discusses and debates until it comes up with a version of American history that it finds persuasive. It does not feel obligated to convince the rest of the historical profession—many of whom are unsympathetic to its views. As long as it is "viable" it can get its version incorporated into American history texts, monographs, conferences, and graduate school seminars. Discussion and debate do not occur within the historical profession as a whole but within the sub-groups. Himmelfarb calls it "the fragmentation of history."

Is this fragmentation caused only by a series of painful memories of how white, Anglo-Saxon Protestant, male historians have omitted or distorted the histories of other racial, ethnic, religious and gender groups? Do these groups write their own histories because they no longer trust historians belonging to other groups? If so, then this fragmentation is certainly understandable considering the past omissions and distortions.

To some extent, though, this fragmentation either results from or results in (probably both, and in confusing combinations) a philosophical relativism. For this discussion, relativism can be defined as the belief that all historical accounts are inherently subjective and necessarily lacking in objectivity.[2]

Cushing Strout has observed, "a consistent relativism is a form of intellectual suicide."[3] Like suicide, it is also accompanied by intellectual despair, a feeling that historical research and writing only add up in the end to a series of entries in the historian's diary, a mere record of the historian's private biases and prejudices that some researcher will easily discover, dissect, and then denounce to later generations of readers.

THE LINGUISTIC CRISIS (THE DECONSTRUCTION) OF HISTORY

Not satisfied to only cast doubt on the objectivity of the historian's interpretations of the past, philosophical relativism now questions whether his or her *words* have any fixed or objective meaning. The second element in the crisis within the historical profession is the linguistic problem, what Himmelfarb calls "the deconstruction of history."

The denial of a fixed meaning in words themselves—deconstruction—began within the field of literary criticism. One literary critic has defined it as follows: "Deconstruction, as it has come to be called, refuses to identify the force of literature with any concept of embodied meaning."[4] Those theories which claim that meaning is embodied in the text he calls "logocentric or incarnationist perspectives."

Writing in the same collection of essays, another critic describes "a thoroughgoing linguistic nihilism, which in its most refined form is the mode now called Deconstruction." If nihilism is defined as "the denial of the existence of any basis for knowledge or truth," then surely the denial of an intrinsic or embodied meaning in words is a form of nihilism. Still another author in this book admits that the nihilistic philosopher Friedrich Nietzsche "is one of the patrons" of "the present-day procedure of 'deconstruction.'"

Deconstruction is best illustrated by the quotation that began this essay—the one about poststructuralists, "signifiers" and "signifieds." Harlan describes what happens when scholars conclude they are "left with an endless chain of signifiers in which meaning is always deferred and finally absent." First, the writer's intended meaning no longer limits or controls what the reader sees as the meaning of the text. Any reader's interpretation is just as authoritative as the author's. Second, the text does not have its own unique meaning, but it has many possible meanings, maybe an infinite number of them. Third, the historian is therefore free to edit the author's words or invent new ones in order to make the author's ideas more relevant to modern society.

This is relativism gone mad, but what is most interesting is Harlan's resort to religious language in describing deconstruction. In Harlan's metaphor, the text becomes a prodigal son and the author its father:

> that every text, at the very moment of its inception, has already been cast onto the waters, that no text can ever hope to rejoin its father, that it is the fate of every text to take up the wanderings of a prodigal son that does not return.

He summarizes another author's contention "that the entire history of Western criticism has been an argument between Jews and Christians over the hope of finding God in his Word, the author in his text." He writes of a secular body of "canonical works" that is now in dispute.

Harlan uses this religious language only as metaphor. What he does not see is the literal application of religious truth to this modern dilemma.

In the course of his argument, Harlan cites a story from the oral traditions of Rabbinic Judaism:

> Finally, there is the wonderful story of Rabbi Eliezer's quarrel with the Sages about the oven of Aknai. When God cried out, "Why do ye dispute with Rabbi Eliezer, seeing that in all matters the *halachah* agrees with him," Rabbi Jeremiah replied, "The Torah has already been given at Mount Sinai; we pay no attention to a Heavenly Voice." At which point God "laughed with joy" and conceded, "My sons have defeated Me, My sons have defeated Me."

This story is used to draw a parallel between Rabbinic concepts concerning "the Word" and modern scholarly concepts concerning the text: both stress "the promise of *multiple* meaning, an invitation to continual interpretation and reinterpretation." Yet there is a difference. The rabbis believed that the Torah had been divinely given at Sinai, whereas most modern scholars have no such belief about the texts they examine.

Harlan does not see that, in the case of the modern scholar, it might be God Who is playing the joke. It might be He Who has defeated them.

We can view the current deconstruction of texts from the secular canon as the end of a process that began in the 19th century with the Higher Criticism "deconstructing" the biblical texts that are the Judeo-Christian canon. We can view current talk of "the death of the author" as a consequence of earlier attempts to argue away God's ultimate "authorship" of the Scriptures. Just as critical scholars have long denied any divine, authoritative intention in the Scriptures, so they no longer see secular authors' intentions as authoritative.

Turnabout is fair play. Modern man has attempted to render meaningless God's Word, so now deconstructionist critics are rendering meaningless the words of every modern (and premodern) author. Harlan's metaphorical observation sounds like a divine sentence imposed on unbelief: "It is the fate of every text to take up the wanderings of a prodigal son that does not return."

There are scriptural passages that would indicate some such divine judgment is at least possible. The Apostle Paul speaks of the futility of human wisdom apart from God:

> Where is the wise man? Where is the scholar?
> Where is the philosopher of this age?
> Has not God made foolish the wisdom of this world?

He quotes the prophet Isaiah who pronounces God's judgment: "'I will destroy the wisdom of the wise; the intelligence of the intelligent I will frustrate'" (1 Corinthians 1:19, 21a).

At the Tower of Babel, God acted to humble human pretensions: "Come, let us go down and confuse their language so they will not understand each other" (Genesis 11:7). Surely deconstruction represents a confusion of language. According to Harlan, deconstruction theory results in "only the incessant and unremitting play of signifiers . . . words become protean and uncontrollable." The prophet Jeremiah writes,

> The wise will be put to shame;
> they will be dismayed and trapped.

Since they have rejected the word of the Lord,
what kind of wisdom do they have? (Jeremiah 8:9)

What kind of wisdom can be achieved by deconstruction? If texts are forever running away from their authors, can they be reliable messengers bringing wisdom or understanding to the reader?

THE LOGOCENTRIC CHRISTIAN, AND THE HISTORIANS' CRISES

Thankfully, the Christian believer need not suffer confusion of language or fragmentation of history. Harlan reports the deconstructionists' view that "there is no external point of reference, no ultimate word, no 'transcendental signified' that will ground meaning, guaranteeing it once and for all." The Christian believer knows otherwise. There is "an ultimate word":

> In the beginning was the Word, and the Word was with God, and the Word was God. He was with God in the beginning . . . . The Word became flesh and made his dwelling among us. We have seen his glory, the glory of the One and Only, who came from the Father, full of grace and truth. (John 1:1–2, 14)

That Word is Jesus Christ, the Eternal Son of God. In describing Him as the Word, the Apostle John used the Greek word *logos*, which the Greeks used to refer to reason as well as to the written or spoken word.

That is not a smug, simplistic answer.

Christians approach these questions with admittedly (and literally) "logocentric or incarnationist perspectives."[5] Our faith is centered on the Logos and His incarnation. Christ is God's message to the world: "In the past God spoke to our forefathers through the prophets . . . but in these last days he has spoken to us by his Son" (Hebrews 1:1). He is God's wisdom, God's reasoning, as well as a specific message. He has "become for us wisdom from God" (1 Corinthians 1:30).[5]

There is a "transcendental signified" and that is God Himself. He is the "ultimate idea or object for which" words and languages can be made to stand. Does He "ground meaning, guaranteeing it?" We know and believe that He does—through Christ, Who is active "sustaining all things by his powerful word" (Hebrews 1:3) and in Whom "all things hold together" (Colossians 1:17). Does He do so "once and for all?" He affirms, "Heaven and earth will pass away, but my words will never pass away" (Luke 21:33). For the Christian believer, this linguistic crisis does not exist.

Our faith in the Logos enables us to confidently endure the taunts of the relativists who say that no "transcendental signified," no "ultimate idea or object" can exist.

Relativism is like the giant in the fairy tale, who sits by the side of the road, asks all passersby the same riddle, and imprisons all who cannot give the correct answer. Because you cannot know everything, or cannot know one thing fully, or cannot state what you know with complete accuracy and objectivity—the giant says—you are condemned to sit and listen to yourselves talk endlessly with no certain meaning. But the answer to the riddle is plain. There is One who knows fully and speaks authoritatively. He has revealed Himself and we can imperfectly pattern ourselves after Him. That is enough for now. "Now I know in part; then I shall know fully, even as I am fully known" (1 Corinthians 13:12b).

Insofar as the revolt against objectivity is a revolt against the narrow, technical rationality of the scientist, engineer, economist or historian—a rationality that excludes human emotional, aesthetic, and spiritual needs—then it is an understandable revolt.

We are seeing the increasing triumph of this tough-minded rationality in American society in the 1980s and 1990s. We see it in terse TV commercials which often feature a team of MBAs sitting around a conference table, meeting deadlines, and tossing off clipped phrases: "Graphics—that's the bottom line," or "Let's cashflow it first." We see it on the MacNeil-Lehrer News Hour when the Salomon Brothers' investment analyst declares with finality that increased spending on inner city neighborhoods will lower market incentives and reduce investor confidence.

Insofar as women sometimes perceive this objectivity as an expression of uncomprehending masculine domination, then it is an understandable revolt. This rationality has narrowed multi-faceted humanity down to a "short list" of quantifiable questions to which it can give short, clipped answers.

That is not the Logos revealed in the Christian gospel. When God took on human form, He did not clothe Himself in a Brooks Brothers suit, nor did He analyze people with unsympathetic and uncomprehending objectivity. He was poor. When He was asked to pay a tax amounting to only two days' wages, He had to perform a miracle to get the money out of a fish's mouth. Presumably, He did not have the cash on hand. He wept at the death of a friend. He "had compassion on" the crowds "because they were harassed and helpless" (Matthew 9:35–36). Sensitive to the need for privacy, He healed a deaf and mute man "away from the crowd" (Mark 7:33). He started a fire and cooked breakfast for His followers while they were out fishing. He did not expect to be waited on, but instead washed His followers' feet. Jewish male religious leaders did not normally hold private conversations with women, but He did.

Since we have a Logos Who is both compassionate and accurate, let us reject both the narrow rationality and the nihilistic deconstructionism that revolts against it. I can remember sitting

130

in a University conference room, listening to a deconstructionist paper on immigrant literature while the sun was setting, and—so deep was the intellectual gloom in the room—wondering whether the presenter was going to sit down or jump out the window when he finished. Christians have a word of hope to speak. There is an "ultimate word . . . that will ground meaning, guaranteeing it once and for all." That Word is Jesus Christ. Let us proclaim Him.

To those who are in intellectual doubt and confusion, the divine message is clear, hopeful, authoritative: "'This is my Son, whom I love. Listen to him!'" (Mark 9:7b).

The fragmentation of history is a more difficult problem. Certainly, it would be a serious mistake to equate a Christian view of history with political conservatism, elitism, Anglo-Saxonism, or antiquarianism. The Christian ought to have no difficulty with recent demands that women, minorities, and lower-class Americans be adequately represented in the story of America's past. They have been made in God's image just as surely as have the more elite actors traditionally overrepresented in that story. Christianity is a cosmopolitan and universal faith, that has served to unite the faithful of all races and classes and of both genders: "There is neither Jew nor Greek, slave nor free, male nor female, for you are all one in Christ Jesus" (Galatians 3:28). The Christian must use this sense of unity in Christ to see the history of other races, of other classes, or of the other gender, as important. Non-Christians do not have this unity of mutual forgiveness to heal grievances over past misrepresentations.

Evangelical Christians ought to use their unique perspective in order to reconsider their own views on American history in light of this fragmentation. Many of us still cling to outmoded, inaccurate, discredited views of the American past. We need not feel obligated to defend the old, consensus view which stressed politics and presidential administrations and America's inevitable progress. That is not a Christian view.

We ought to develop our own interpretation(s). We ought to heed the Apostle Paul's advice, and "take captive every thought to make it obedient to Christ" (2 Corinthians 10:5b). With their lack of attention to religious phenomena and their lack of understanding of them, secular historians write American history in a way that undercuts the Christian apologetic. Their interpretation often "sets itself up against the knowledge of God." Turnabout is fair play. We ought to use American history to undercut the secular apologetic.

Our own interpretation is in itself no answer to the philosophical attacks on historical objectivity. What enables the Christian believer to escape both this relativism and fragmentation is the knowledge that a complete, fair, objective and accurate account of human history does exist—in the mind of God. Historian Arthur S. Link made this point clearly:

> The historical record . . . is stored in its incredible totality in the mind and memory of God . . . the historian, while acknowledging that only God knows all historical truth, can now affirm, profess, and confess that he stands in the presence of something . . . that gives meaning to his life and work—the faith and knowledge that every single fact of history has its own objective existence and integrity.[6]

This faith in an omniscient God who does not show favoritism but judges all impartially enables us to forget and forgive past misrepresentations because the final historical verdict will be fair and full. Furthermore, this will not be a verdict rendered by a God unaquainted with human temptations, privation or suffering. In Jesus Christ, the divine nature has experienced what human nature has to endure. The Logos is both compassionate and accurate. Who will be able to defy His logic or question His love?

17

A QUIET LIFE,
NOT JUST A QUIET TIME

The lives of too many Christians are best described in these lines by the English poet William Wordsworth:

> The world is too much with us; late and soon,
> Getting and spending, we lay waste our powers:
> Little we see in Nature that is ours;
> We have given our hearts away, a sordid boon![1]

We might not capitalize and idolize nature as this early 19th century Romantic did. We might have a more biblical understanding of "the world." Yet the predicament is the same.

We *must* read the morning newspaper each day, listen to drive-time radio, follow the daily doings of each of our city's professional sports teams, keep up with Wall Street, keep informed of upcoming cultural events and attend several each month, and read one weekly newsmagazine to stay current.

Is any one of these activities harmful? Probably not, but the cumulative effect can be devastating upon urban Christians who feel they must stay current on everything in order to communicate effectively with others.

We become like the college students who bring with them to class those large, plastic soft-drink containers with the plastic straws already attached. If they only knew they looked like infants carrying bottles. They seem also to be perpetually nursing from the world's flow of current styles, current slang, and current attitudes. As Christians, we can become similarly dependent.

We gradually acquire the world's viewpoint, which is inextricably embedded in the daily bombardment of information. Here's a test. After reading newsmagazine articles about the Baby Boom generation, reading demographic data on their buying habits, and watching "thirtysomething," how easy is it to pronounce these words:

> O unbelieving and perverse generation (Jesus);
> Save yourselves from this corrupt generation (Peter);
> . . . a crooked and depraved generation?" (Paul)
> (Matthew 17:17; Acts 2:40b; Philippians 2:15b)

Gradually we come to believe that this generation is maturing, questioning, less prosperous than its parents' generation, the perpetual center of national attention—but not perverse, corrupt or depraved. Those words seem stranger the more we read, listen, and watch the media reports. We have imperceptibly accepted the world's opinion of itself: it is aging, anxious and maybe less affluent, but certainly not crooked or corrupt.

The remedy for this conformity to the world is supposed to be the daily Quiet Time, perhaps a half-hour alone reading the Word and praying. But can a mind that is conformed to the world for sixteen waking hours be transformed in 30 minutes? Doesn't the biblical passage just become one more input among many? Or, instead of transforming our whole life, does it only have the limited effect of reinforcing the desire for another daily Quiet Time tomorrow? Why not a Quiet Life, instead of just a Quiet Time?

Perhaps a rural perspective can be helpful. It is primarily urban culture that incessantly works to make a Quiet Life seem impossible. Can the rural experience speak to American society, and to America's urban Christians? The very idea may seem strange and nostalgic.

As we are approaching the point where 75% of the American people will be classified as urban and only 25% as rural, we are certainly long past the point where American culture became urban-oriented. The books, poems, plays, and articles produced by our high culture, and the TV sit-coms, rock music, movies and videos produced by our popular culture are strongly urban in their subject matter and their perspective. Even what we consider "country" writing—usually essays or poetry written on rural themes—is most often done in country settings by exiled urbanites or by urbanites just traveling through. Even this "country" writing represents urban attitudes, the writers often romanticizing the countryside or occasionally denigrating it, but in either case from an implicitly urban perspective.

So great is the urban cultural domination that it would surprise many Americans to have it called domination, or to have it questioned. Isn't it inevitable for urban people to do the brainwork, while rural people serve as hewers of wood and drawers of water? How can the out-dated rural experience have anything to teach urban Americans or urban Christians?

Well, how might the rural mind usefully critique American culture? It might look for substance and not be fooled by a pleasing style. It might be concise, using the proverbs and aphorisms that have long appealed to rural people. It might not be taken in by the philosophy of relativism, since the difference between truth and error is plain in the country and the consequences of both are clear. It might stress character and integrity, since both are necessary in order to maintain a good reputation under the scrutinizing eyes and in the long memories of neighbors. It might not romanticize, for the rural mind sees things as they are, not as someone wishes they could be.

Such a rural critique might be useful. But not very useful.

In its natural condition, the rural mind is also separated from God. Shrewdness sits around the tables in the small-town coffeeshops—a kind of horse trader's shrewdness that knows how to size up people, land, animals, or machinery and how to get the most out of them all. Shrewdness in small matters. It knows how to get the upper hand in a deal but doesn't know how unimportant it is to beat your neighbor in a deal. It judges by what can be seen, not by what is unseen. Thus, it is shortsighted, "for what is seen is temporal, but what is unseen is eternal" (2 Corinthians 4:18b). It lacks the faith to believe that changed lives are possible. If this husband has been unfaithful or a drunkard, then he will always be that way. If that mother has neglected her children, then she will continue to do so. This rural shrewdness doesn't really believe in the life-changing Gospel of Jesus Christ.

A foolish, romanticizing concept runs like a thread throughout American history—the belief that rural means virtuous. Often called Jeffersonian, it was most clearly asserted by Thomas Jefferson. Here are two Jeffersonian texts:

> Those who labour in the earth are the chosen people of God, if ever he had a chosen people, whose breasts he has made his peculiar deposit for substantial and genuine virtue .... Corruption of morals in the mass of cultivators is a phænomenon of which no age nor nation has furnished an example. (1)

> The cultivators of the earth are the most virtuous citizens, and possess most of the amor patriae.[2] (2)

The second quote represents Jefferson's praise for the citizens of Connecticut (mostly farmers) who he contrasted to the scoundrels in Rhode Island (mostly merchants). Unfortunately for his thesis regarding Connecticut farmers' love of country, they were notorious during the American Revolution for withholding foodstuffs from the Continental Army until the price went higher. The first quote calling farmers "the chosen people of God" is a bold overstatement that only a Founding Father could get away with. Certainly, most Christians would disagree: Israel is God's chosen people, and corruption of morals is possible among any people.

Current problems of child abuse, alcoholism, drug abuse, and marital infidelity in rural areas prove conclusively that corruption of morals is possible in the countryside and that the words "rural" and "virtue" are not synonyms.

Apart from the Christian faith, the rural mind cannot accurately critique American culture. Only a rural perspective shaped by the Gospel can be of any benefit—and we can find that perspective in the Gospel accounts themselves.

Our Lord was from the small rural village of Nazareth in the rich agricultural region called Galilee. Eleven of the twelve apostles He chose were from Galilee (all except Judas Iscariot). There is evidence in the Gospels to indicate that both He and they were despised partly because of their rural, Galilean origins. When Philip told Nathanael about Jesus of Nazareth, Nathanael replied "Nazareth! Can anything good come from there?" (John 1:46a). When Nicodemus tried to defend Jesus before his fellow Pharisees,

> They replied, "Are you from Galilee, too? Look into it, and you will find that a prophet does not come out of Galilee." (John 7:52)

Galileans were despised by the religious authorities in Jerusalem, and looked down on by the inhabitants of Judea.[3] They mispronounced Hebrew and made grammatical mistakes when writing it. A common saying was "Galilean—Fool!" We can surely infer some irony in the amazed cry of the audience which heard the apostles speak in foreign languages on Pentecost: "Are not all these men who are speaking Galileans?" (Acts 2:7b).

In sending the Messiah and His apostles out from despised Galilee to proud, self-assured Judea, God

> chose the lowly things of this world and the despised things—and the things that are not—to nullify the things that are, so that no one may boast before him. (1 Corinthians 1:28–29)

Many rural people can testify that there is a pecking order of place-names, just as there was in first-century Palestine. The resident of Manhattan looks down on the visitor from Cleveland, who in turn looks down on the person from Dayton—and so on down the line until the resident of the smallest county seat in Ohio comes to despise the "hicks" from the outlying towns and villages in that county, and the storekeeper in the smallest outlying village still sees himself as superior in some way to the farmer living on the back roads.

From the bottom, the rural resident can see how un-Christian that pecking order is, and yet how typical of "the world." He can critique the pride and boasting that lies behind it. He can perhaps see the truth of the Apostle John's definition of the world: "the cravings of sinful man, the lust of his eyes and the boasting of what he has and does" (1 John 2:16b). And the boasting of where he lives! The rural resident is at least delivered from the worldliness of boasting of where he lives. If he thinks a little, he will see what a powerful statement of opposition to the world God made when He sent His Son from such a despised place as Nazareth in Galilee.

Apart from the Gospel, however, he can not abstain from loving the world, because there is a rural "world" as well as an urban one. He can only feel resentment that his "world" is looked down on by lovers of that urban world. Only the Gospel can convince anyone of the folly of the cravings, the lust and the boasting occurring in all places.

There is that rural shrewdness that stands in the way of rural people coming to accept the Gospel. Far from understanding the amazing honor bestowed on their despised village, Nazareth's people used their rural shrewdness to completely reject the Gospel when Jesus returned to preach:

> "Where did this man get these things?" they asked. "What's this wisdom that has been given him, that he even does miracles? Isn't this the carpenter? Isn't this Mary's son and the brother of James, Joseph, Judas and Simon? Aren't his sisters here with us?" And they took offense at him. (Mark 6:2b–3)

Nazareth's folly is repeated in many rural areas, as shrewd, practical people ignore or oppose the work that God is trying to do in their midst.

Having accepted the Gospel and repented of short-sighted shrewdness, the rural Christian, however, can use rural residence as a weaning from the world. The TVs, VCRs and cable channels available in rural areas make living in a rural area no longer an automatic separation from "the world." Separation takes some willpower too.

I remember moving to rural Minnesota twelve years ago—the almost physical feeling of isolation. I used to walk two miles down a dirt road to stand by the interstate highway to watch the cars whiz by and to dream of being connected—to restaurants, to resorts, to sophisticated dinner table conversations, to interesting people and entertaining cultural events. It took years for the weaning process to work, for the pain of longing to disappear—but it's worth it! It's not just the stars and the sunsets that seem more clearly visible in the country. If we truly desire it, the Lord can also seem more clearly visible.

In one of his short, simple Psalms, David expressed it best:

> My heart is not proud, O Lord,
> my eyes are not haughty;
> I do not concern myself with great matters
> or things too wonderful for me.
> But I have stilled and quieted my soul;
> like a weaned child with its mother,
> like a weaned child is my soul within me.
> (Psalm 131:1–2)

It is only as the soul has been weaned from the world that it can be truly filled with a sense of the majesty, grace and goodness of God.

That is the perspective that the rural Christian can offer. The cravings, the lust, the boasting, the race for knowledge and power—all is useless. Moving out of the city to chase a romanticized vision of the country is also useless, a chasing after the wind. The peaceful countryside is not what it seems.

To paraphrase the apostle Paul, those who live in the city should live as if they did not; they should live a Quiet Life, weaned from the world. Those who live in the country should live as if they did not; the repeating seasonal cycles of nature that seem so eternal and unchanging will not continue forever—"the time is short"—"this world in its present form is passing away" (1 Corinthians 7:29–31). They must not seek a delusive peace among the pines. They must be sure that the quietness in their lives is not merely an absence of street noise, but an absence of pride and haughtiness and the *presence* of the Lord.

Whether in the country or the city, a Quiet Life is possible, but only for the weaned child.

18

JEHOVAH'S SOLE DEFENDER

His brothers' taunts still sounding in his ear—
"No public figure acts in secret here,"
On dusty trails from despised Galilee,
Against a biting wind, He walks to Judea.
Dependent on friends' hospitality,
Without drachmas to pay the Roman tax,
He leads a few followers whom He asked
To defy Tiberius' empire—
Well knowing when the final crisis came
They'd flee, deny, warm their hands by the fire.

He walks an unknown, spiritual way
Those who walk alongside Him cannot see:
Showing by submission his authority,
Claiming a spiritual kingdom by
Leaving those who would proclaim Him their king,
Concealing that He was their Messiah—
The word's new meaning would be His making.
Out-numbered, Messiah yet pariah,
Rejecting those who would give allegiance,

He accepts and loves His own betrayer.

Jericho—we sit like Bartimaeus
As this Atlas walks by for the last time
On His way to turn the world upside down.
"Have mercy!" we cry—the crowd yells, "Sit down!"
To sit or stand—we're suspended in doubt
'Til the trumpets' sound, the archangel's shout.

19

PRISONERS OF HOPE

One summer, we attended a Bible conference at Grove City college in Pennsylvania. It rained all week long. The fog and rainy mists seemed like the weather's attempt to give observable form to spiritual forces, to set the scene for a spiritual drama, which occurred each dark night in the large auditorium. The drama was without a hint of entertainment, for what hung in the balance was not Willy Loman's life or Laura's fragile psyche, but the eternal fate of one's own soul. Each one present a tragic hero or heroine, and the line between good and evil running down the middle of each soul.

It was darkest night, Passover night, and vast crowds flocked through the streets—bearing slain lambs on staves laid on their shoulders—knocking on doors to ask for an upper room where they could celebrate Passover—after the closing Hallel hymn, hastening to the moon-lit Temple, its marble walls 15 stories high, its gates now swinging open at midnight to admit entering pilgrims and priests preparing for the morning sacrifice. The Teacher predicted His betrayal. "Is it I?" the disciples asked. After betrayal and interrogation, beating and mockery, the question was asked, "What shall I do, then, with the one you call the king of the Jews?" Millions of individual eternities hung in the balance. The King became the morning sacrifice amidst a cosmic drama—darkness at noon, the veil of the Temple torn.

The ancient public drama presently forces an individual moment of decision in the college auditorium, as the closing hymn is sung.

> Have you any room for Jesus,
> He who bore your load of sin?
> As He knocks and asks admission,
> Sinner, will you let Him in?
> Room for Jesus, King of glory!
> Hasten now, His word obey;
> Swing the heart's door widely open,
> Bid Him enter while you may.[1]

When I was a child going to Sunday meeting, we sat in old-fashioned backed benches arranged in a square, with a simple linen-covered table in the center of the square. No priest or pastor commanded our attention from the front. There was no obvious leader whose performance we were assembled to witness and comment on afterwards. There were no portraits on the wall—no artistic indication of who it was we were there to honor. No one rewarded us for having attended this meeting, called the Remembrance meeting. Its purpose was to remember someone whom we had never seen, to commemorate the death of someone whom we had not known before His death. It recalled a Passover at which, reclining around a low table, the Head of the Company and the Twelve ate the unleavened bread, the bitter herbs, the wine mixed with water, and the Passover Lamb. Now, the intimacy of a supper was present, though the Head of the Company was seemingly absent, and no one else presumed to serve as leader in His absence. Guests met without any apparent host.

On Sunday afternoon or evening, a traveling preacher or teacher might be invited to open the Word, read a passage, and interpret it. Like a first-century synagogue, this meeting hall had no altar—just a large, sparsely-furnished meeting room with a raised platform, from which the teacher spoke.[2] This was indeed a religion of the Book, and not of ritual or sacrifice—though, unlike first-century Galilee, that was not because of distance from the Temple where rituals were observed and sacrifices made, but because the Sacrifice had been made once and for all. The lack of ceremony and the absence of anything for the eye to feast on—all drove the imagination deep into the Book. We could see the traveling Teacher who visited the Capernaum synagogue, took the scroll, read a passage, and interpreted it for the assembly. Like the others, we also were amazed that He spoke with authority. Afterwards, He ate at Simon's house and we went to our cousins' house for Sunday dinner.

Once each summer these meetings took place at a camp by a lakeshore. After the meeting ended, we might walk down to the shore and along the beach, past the idle boats drawn up on shore, with the lake breeze in our faces—thinking about a distant seashore we had never seen, with fishing boats along its beach, nets drying, incoming waves erasing crowds of footprints from the sand, and a stiff breeze blowing Aramaic words to shore. We felt clean, as if newly created, and yet with memories centuries old.

> O when shall the mists be removed,
> And round us Thy brightness be poured?
> When meet Thee, whom absent we've loved,
> When see, whom unseen we've adored?[3]

From the sidewalk along Fourth Street S.E., we entered a former Masonic hall that had been converted into Campus Church. No seats were left in the second-floor auditorium for the Sunday morning service. We stood at one third-floor window looking for friends in the congregation below and waiting for the Pastor with his soft Northern Irish brogue. We were like Judeans listening to the strange dialect of the Galilean, crowding in, standing and looking on from a distant window because the inner courtyard was full, come to hear teaching with authority. Hundreds were singing,

> Son of God, what a wonder you are,
> Son of God, what a wonder you are . . .[4]

How can someone unseen be so real that it seems like He is knocking and that you can let Him in? An historical memory, a dim glimpse of the past, does not seem that real. The Apostle Peter wrote to 1st century believers of their faith in Yeshua the Messiah:

> Though you have not seen him, you love him; and even though you do not see him now, you believe in him and are filled with an inexpressible and glorious joy. (1 Peter 1:8)

The Apostle Paul saw Him as a blinding "physical" light, but we perceive Him more as a brilliant emotional brightness Who fills us with "an inexpressible and glorious joy." Like concentrating the rays of the sun on one spot with a magnifying glass, different lines of thought are focused on one Person: Son of God and Son of Man; God's love and God's justice met; priest, prophet and king in one Person. Bright enough is each line by itself. The point where each meet becomes blindingly brilliant. Especially so, because the meeting is seemingly impossible—like two parallel lines converging at one point. Seemingly, parallel lines can never meet, nor can the Creator be standing helpless before mocking Roman soldiers or hanging helpless while He bears the punishment for twentieth century sins. All of the terrible and wonderful paradoxes of the Gospel meet in Him:

> God made Him Who had no sin to be a sin offering for us,
> so that in Him we might become the righteousness of God.
> (2 Corinthians 5:21)

> Christ redeemed us from the curse of the law by ecoming a curse
> for us, for it is written, "Cursed is everyone who is hung on a
> tree." (Galatians 3:13)

When we meet Him and believe in Him we too become personally involved in these paradoxes and seeming contradictions. We walk through late 20th century Minnesota with memories of a 1st century Jewish carpenter named Yeshua, who followed none of the rules by which one would normally try to be acclaimed a King or to establish a Kingdom. We proclaim as King One who was crucified by order of a Roman provincial governor.

> Jesus looked directly at them and asked, Then what is the
> meaning of that which is written: "The stone that the builders
> rejected has become the cornerstone?" (Luke 20:17)

He was quoting a passage from Psalm 118 (verse 22), a verse from the closing Hallel hymn which He would later sing after His Supper and before His crucifixion.

He quoted and sang a paradox. The rejected stone is the cornerstone. And He set us, His followers, in direct opposition to the builders, to the authorities.

Listen to what the authorities say. The Roman official, Pliny the Younger, in 111 A.D. called Christians, "this wretched cult," that "met regularly before dawn on a fixed day to chant verses alternately amongst themselves in honor of Christ as if to a god." Here we are—like those 2nd century Christians whom the Roman satirist Lucian ridiculed:

These lunatics believe that they are immortal and will live forever, so that they do not fear death and willingly accept arrest. Deluded by their original lawgiver, they believe that they are all brothers once they have . . . worshiped that crucified sophist and accepted his laws.

We have become like the women Thomas Jefferson ridiculed, with "their night meetings and praying parties, where, attended by their priests, and sometimes by a hen-pecked husband, they pour forth the effusions of their love to Jesus."[5]

Our Creator God has set up an absolute contradiction between human plans and His own plans, between human kingdoms and His own Kingdom, between the *verdensby* and His City. He has personified this contradiction in the Person of Christ and ensured that the contradictory views would eventually collide. "The stone that the builders rejected has become the cornerstone."

There is no way of compromising this contradiction, of somehow splitting the difference or negotiating a way out.

We Christians, believers in the One whom the authorities call "that crucified sophist," have placed ourselves on one side of this vast contradiction hurrying towards the collision that is called apocalypse. Our Lord has placed us on a collision course with the world around us—for the collision is interpersonal as well as cosmic. We are like witnesses at a trial testifying against our own friends, neighbors and relatives—and they against us. Charges of perjury hang over their heads and ours. Our lives testify that theirs are false, and their lives attempt to testify that ours are false. In day-to-day conversation we attempt to downplay this contradiction with soft words about different lifestyles, by small compromises and by silence at strategic moments. Our Western culture seeks to downplay it by creating a private world of values for those who choose to believe that Jesus Christ is Lord, while denying that fact in the public world.

But we honor Him who was not silent or compromising about His intention to turn the world upside down: the last shall be first; the great must become servant of all; he who finds his life shall lose it and he who loses his life will find it.

So we are caught up in His paradoxes. We do not even know exactly what we will become: "now we are children of God, and what we will be has not yet been made known. But we know that when He appears, we shall be like Him, for we shall see Him as He is" (1 John 3:2b).

We are prisoners of hope. We will sit down and drink the wine with the Head of the Company present and leading the service, in the congregation of congregations. We shall see Him Whom unseen we've adored. Most amazingly, the One Who has seen us all along will still adore us. "He will see the result of the suffering of His soul and be satisfied" (Isaiah 53:11a, NIV alternate reading). And we will be satisfied with that Person in Whom all the lines of grace and truth brilliantly meet.

NOTES

SERIOUS MISCALCULATIONS

1. The descriptions of the Cane Ridge Revival are taken from Paul K. Conkin, *Cane Ridge: America's Pentecost* (Madison: University of Wisconsin Press, 1990), pp. 94, 114.

THAT SCARECROW WORD, FUNDAMENTALISM

1. Information on the early twentieth-century publication of *The Fundamentals* is taken from C. Allyn Russell, *Voices of American Fundamentalism: Seven Biographical Sketches* (Philadelphia: Westminster Press, 1976), pp. 16–19.

2. For Barr's criticisms of fundamentalism, see James Barr, *Fundamentalism* (Philadelphia: Westminster Press, 1978), pp. 36–37, 313.

THE FOUR PRINCIPLES OF THE APOCALYPSE

1. "The World's Last Night" is found in C. S. Lewis, *The World's Last Night and Other Essays* (New York: Harcourt, Brace & World, 1960). The quoted passage is on page 93.

2. For the Millerites, their mathematics, and the millenium, see George Brown Tindall, *America: A Narrative History* (New York: W. W. Norton, 1984), vol. 1, pp. 474–475.

3. In quoting from Isaiah 52:14–15a, I have chosen the New International Version's alternate reading, which is based on the Septuagint.

4. The quotes from Lesslie Newbigin are taken from Lesslie

Newbigin, *Foolishness to the Greeks: The Gospel and Western Culture* (Grand Rapids: William B. Eerdmans Publishing Company, 1986), pp. 14, 19, 134.

JOURNEY INTO THE INTERIOR OF DENMARK AND NORWAY

1. The excerpt from the 1990–91 edition of Copenhagen's telephone book is by Kirsten Toxværd and is entitled "Oplevelser i City."

2. N. F. S. Grundtvig's hymn, "Denne er dagen some Herren har gjort," is the hymn in Vor Frue Kirke's hymnal. I accept responsibility for this rather literal and unpoetic translation.

3. Information about Olaf Haraldsson is taken from Gwyn Jones, *A History of the Vikings* (London: Oxford University Press, 1968), pp. 375–378, 385; and from Thorkild Ramskou, *Danmarks Historie: Normannertiden, 600–1060* (København: Politikens Forlag, 1962), pp. 455–457.

4. John R. W. Stott, *The Cross of Christ* (Downers Grove: InterVarsity Press, 1986).

5. Kierkegaard's comment on infant baptism is taken from Bent Hylleberg and Bjarne Miller Jørgensen, *Et kirkesamfund bliver til: Danske baptisters historie gennem 150 År* (København: Føltveds Forlag, 1989), p. 56.

6. Svend B. Johnsen comments on the low church attendance in Denmark in an article ("Er folkekirken døende?") in *Berlingske Tidende* that was reprinted in *Church and Life* (Askov), vol. 34, no. 6 (15 June 1985), pp. 3–5.

7. The article on Fukuyama's piece appeared in the Opinion section (p. 8) of *Weekendavisen* on August 11, 1989.

SETTING ASIDE GOD'S COMMANDS TO OBSERVE TRADITIONS

1. Especially helpful in defining the false gospel of civil religion and in providing historical examples was Richard V. Pierard & Robert D. Linder, *Civil Religion & the Presidency* (Grand Rapids: Zondervan, 1988).

See especially pp. 48–56 and 294.

2. Torbjorn Greipsland reports King Olav's remark about Jesus' Second Coming in "Kong Olav V: Helhjertet innsats for kirke og misjon," reprinted in *Western Viking*, 25 January 1991, p. 10.

3. Quotes from *Utopia* are taken from the H. V. S. Ogden translation (New York: Appleton-Century-Crofts, 1949), pp. 70–71.

4. Hector St. John de Crevecoeur's *Letters from an American Farmer* are excerpted in Marvin Meyers, John G. Cawelti, and Alexander Kern, eds., *Sources of the American Republic: A Documentary History of Politics, Society, and Thought* (Glenview: Scott, Foresman and Company, 1967), vol. 1, especially, p. 283.

5. Turgot is quoted in William B. Wheeler & Susan D. Becker, *Discovering the American Past: A Look at the Evidence* (Boston: Houghton Mifflin, 1990), p. 66.

6. The comparison between Marxism and republicanism, and other facts about republicanism, are taken from Gordon S. Wood's section on early America in Bernard Bailyn, et al., *The Great Republic: A History of the American People*, 4th ed. (Lexington: D. C. Heath and Company, 1992), pp. 273–277.

7. Robert Dallek is the historian who refers to "local values" in Bailyn, et al., *The Great Republic*, p. 365.

8. For Newbigin on freedom, see *Foolishness to the Greeks*, p. 138. Parts of the discussion of Republicans vs. Democrats are taken from my op-ed piece, "Election Lacks Accountability," in *Duluth News-Tribune* (June 1988).

YOUR PAST IS OUR PRESENT

1. Wendell Berry is quoted from his *Home Economics: Fourteen Essays by Wendell Berry* (San Francisco: North Point Press, 1987), pp. 125–126.

2. I have taken the details of the Hanska story from the following sources: Nina Draxten, *Kristofer Janson in America* (Northfield: Norwegian-American Historical Association, 1976); Odd S. Lovoll, *The Promise of America: A History of the Norwegian-American People* (Minneapolis: University of Minnesota Press, 1984), pp. 104–105;

Christian Ahlness, "Recollections of an Emigrant, as Told by Himself," unpublished manuscript, and "Protokol for Lake Hanska Menighed," microfilm copy, both in Brown County Historical Society Museum, New Ulm; and *Budstikken*, 22 August 1883.

3. For Lasch's views, see *The True and Only Heaven*, chapter 2 ("The Idea of Progress Reconsidered") and chapter 3 ("Nostalgia: The Abdication of Memory").

SINCE THEY HAVE REJECTED
THE WORD OF THE LORD

In a very different form, this essay first appeared in *The Crucible: A Journal for Christian Graduate Students* (Winter 1992), pp. 14–17.

1. For David Harlan's essay on "Intellectual History and the Return of History," and Gertrude Himmelfarb's essay, "Some Reflections on the New History," see *American Historical Review*, vol. 94 (June 1989). For the most exhaustive discussion of the "objectivity question" in history, see Peter Novick, *That Noble Dream: The "Objectivity Question" and the American Historical Profession* (Cambridge: Cambridge University Press, 1988).

2. Joan Wallach Scott documents some past historians' biases as shown in past presidential addresses to the American Historical Association in her contribution, "History in Crisis? The Others' Side of the Story," in the June 1989 *AHR*.

3. For the quote from Cushing Strout, and some elementary errors in historical relativism, see David Hackett Fischer, *Historians' Fallacies: Toward a Logic of Historical Thought* (New York: Harper, 1970), pp. 42–43.

4. The critic's definition of deconstruction (by Geoffrey Hartman), one deconstructionist's (Harold Bloom's) reference to nihilism, and another's (J. Hillis Miller's) to Friedrich Nietzsche, are all taken from Harold Bloom, Paul De Man, Jacques Derrida, Geoffrey H. Hartman, and J. Hillis Miller, *Deconstruction & Criticism* (New York: Continuum, 1979), pp. vii., 4, and 229. The definition of nihilism is taken from *Webster's New Twentieth-Century Dictionary of the English Language— Unabridged* (New York: Simon and Schuster, 1983).

5. For an example of a deconstructionist reference to the "incarnationist" perspective, see Geoffrey Hartman's "Preface" in Bloom, et al., *Deconstruction & Criticism*, vii.

6. Ronald H. Nash discusses the possible relationship between Hellenistic philosophers' use of the term *logos* and the New Testament writers' use of that term. See Ronald H. Nash, *Christianity & the Hellenistic World* (Grand Rapids: Zondervan, 1984), pp. 81–112.

6. Arthur S. Link's essay, "The Historian's Vocation," is found in C.T. McIntire, editor, *God, History and Historians: An Anthology of Modern Christian Views of History* (New York: Oxford, 1977).

A QUIET LIFE, NOT JUST A QUIET TIME

1. For the passage from Wordsworth's "The World is Too Much with Us," see Oscar Williams, ed., *Immortal Poems of the English Language: British and American Poetry from Chaucer's Time to the Present Day* (New York: Simon & Schuster, 1952), p. 260.

2. Jefferson's well-known statements on farmers' virtue are taken from his "Notes on the State of Virginia" and from his "Answers and Observations for Demeunier's Article on the United States in the Encyclopædie Methodique, 1786." See Thomas Jefferson, *Writings* (New York: Library of America, 1984), pp. 290, 577.

3. Alfred Edersheim described Judeans' prejudice against Galileans in his *Life and Times of Jesus the Messiah* (Grand Rapids: William B. Eerdmans Publishing Company, 1971), 225–226.

PRISONERS OF HOPE

1. For "Have You Any Room for Jesus?" see Alfred B. Smith, compiler, *Inspiring Hymns: A Choice Selection of Hymns and Gospel Songs for the Singing Church* (Grand Rapids: Zondervan, 1951), number 420.

2. Details concerning first-century customs, synagogues, Temple, and Passover, are taken from Edersheim, *The Life and Times of Jesus the Messiah*.

3. For the hymn "O When Shall the Mists be Removed?" see *A Few*

Hymns and Some Spiritual Songs Selected 1856 for the Little Flock (New York: Loizeau Brothers, 1881 revision), p. 239.

4. The lines "Son of God, What a Wonder You Are," are taken from *Praise Chorus Book* (San Clemente: Maranatha! Music, 1983), number 60.

5. For the quotes from Pliny and Lucian, see Thomas W. Africa, *Rome of the Caesars* (New York: John Wiley & Sons, 1965), pp. 151, 183. Jefferson made his remarks in a letter to Dr. Thomas Cooper, dated 2 November 1922. See Thomas Jefferson, *Writings*, p. 1464.

www.ingramcontent.com/pod-product-compliance
Lightning Source LLC
Chambersburg PA
CBHW021333090426
42742CB00008B/591